The
Happiness
Toolkit

THE SECRETS OF SUCCESS, FULFILMENT
AND FINDING YOUR TRUE SELF

Alexander Butler

Thanks and Acknowledgements

I would like to thank all the people who contributed to this book: all those who donated their energy, time and skills to make it a success.

Thank you to Mike, Kieran, Dom and Suzannah, whose feedback and support has been essential in getting my rambling words into a smart shape and onto the market. Many thanks to my cover designer Svitlana and my interior designer Fabio.

Of course, a massive thank you to all my coaching clients. Thank you for the trust you put in me, and thank you for the courage you bring to our work. You inspire me every day and, frankly, you were the guinea pigs for everything in these pages!

Thank you to all those teachers who showed me the path: Dr Peter Vardy, without whom I would not have taken my first steps away from self-destruction and towards wisdom; Reverend Roy Dorey, who showed me spirituality at work and in service to a community and who I miss so dearly; Mac, the founder of Embercombe, whose powerful rallying call to accountability and personal power shook my heart; Jonathan, who trained me in the arts of grief and who showed me that there are much worse things to fear in life than mere suffering.

To all those who have walked the path beside me, and been treasured sounding boards and (at times) the voices of reason. Here I include Dr Ben, Thom, Sara, Barney, Sue, Sue and M9.

Thank you to my mother, Maddeline and my father, John. Thank you for everything you gave me.

To the gentle waves of my home in Brighton and to the thundering breakers in Iona, where my writing journey began, thank you.

Contents

The journey ahead

Hello and welcome to this series of books about happiness.

My name is Alexander and I'm a Master Life Coach, philosopher and author based in the UK. Every day, I work with coaching clients from all around the world, from all sorts of backgrounds, who bring their own unique challenges and, usually, an urgent need to achieve some kind of change. It's my job to provide that, and I've spent my whole life building up the knowledge and skills that I use in each coaching session.

It's always been very important to me to understand why people do what they do. In a later chapter, I'll share my own journey and the struggles I went through, and you'll understand why I've devoted my life to this topic.

I was raised by a psychotherapist, and I went on to study philosophy, theology and ethics at degree level. From there, I moved into business and community leadership, getting hands-on experience in all sorts of positions, and finally starting to work as a coach in 2009. I was actively studying every possible aspect on the human person alongside whatever work I was doing: psychology, neuroscience, sociology, mythology, a range of spiritual traditions, physical therapies, physical training, martial arts, leadership development, how to organise and empower communities. Since then, I've been intensively working in the field, figuring out what works and what doesn't.

So what you get in this trilogy is a lifetime of dedicated research in the theory and practice of happiness and personal development, rigorously tested in the crucible of the modern world, regularly applied to the challenges my clients bring to their coaching journeys, and proven to be successful. I also personally apply every rule and principle in these books to my own life. It's very important to me to be an authentic leader in my field: I would never ask my clients to do something I wouldn't be willing to do.

My goal in writing these books is to share some of the most important answers I've found through research and clinical practice, and to condense that enormous body of knowledge into a form that's practical and applicable by anyone.

Book 1, which you're currently reading, is about deeply understanding the nature of the problem, and then getting equipped with a toolkit to make meaningful progress. Why are so many people unhappy? What keeps us locked in unhappy places in our lives, unable to progress? How is it that we can end up stuck in unhappy places in our lives? What will free us up and let us build newer, happier lives? What techniques, knowledge and beliefs do you need in order to shake up your life and make it a truly happy place?

I'll begin by telling you about my own journey and how I went from a quiet, confused and shy young man to someone who helps people find purpose in life and who regularly advises CEOs, senior managers and leaders in their field. From there, we'll dive into some core theory: the nature of masks, the idea of *Arete*, the beliefs that lead us to feel trapped or stuck or disempowered in life, we'll explore the nature of true personal strength…and I will steadily equip you with knowledge and tools that will set you up for a life-changing journey of personal development.

While some of this theory might seem dry or abstract at times, I encourage you to constantly bring it back to your own life and your daily experiences. Try to keep returning to questions like:

- Where does this show up in my life?
- How does this affect the choices I make every day?
- Can I see this playing out at work, or in my family, or in my relationships?
- Which of my friends come to mind when I'm reading this?

- Which people in my life are good examples here, who I can try to learn from, and who do I know who embodies the very worst of these traits?

By the end of this book you'll be like a traveller, all set to embark on the road.

The next book, The 12 Rules of Happiness, is the big one. Here you'll find the core lessons, the 12 things that everyone needs to know to create a happy, strong, resilient, successful life. This is where I've really tried to create a set of simple, accessible rules out of a lifetime of learning. The 12 Rules are things you can apply to every aspect of your life. Every massive breakthrough that happens in my coaching sessions is founded on the 12 Rules. They work, and I've got thousands of hours of evidence to prove it.

Book 3 is about integrating these lessons into your life. A great many of my coaching clients have completed powerful journeys of self-mastery, only to find that the way they think and feel, the way they relate to people, and the things they choose to do with their time have all changed. Their old life feels weird, uncomfortable and alien, but they haven't built a new life yet. A lot of people make huge progress in personal development, but then they encounter these feelings and, not knowing what to do with them, they can fall back into their old patterns. This is really common but nobody really talks about it, so book 3 is about integrating your personal development into your life in a practical way.

What kind of happiness?

Happiness can mean a lot of things to a lot of people, and the shape of your happiness will be unique to you. I'll be aiming to help you understand the shape of your own happiness, and then support you to pursue it. It's true that certain habits, certain beliefs and certain information help everyone to reach happiness, no matter what their specific goals are. From there, we'll be getting clearer on what you, personally, need to create a really nourishing, fulfilling, sustainably happy life.

To be clear, however, we are talking about a specific meaning of 'happiness' here. When some people think about happiness they think about an elated state, maybe even a manic state, where all their problems are forgotten because they're too busy being lost in the giddy joy of the moment. We're not seeking that, here. The Webster dictionary defined happiness as:

Happiness. Noun.

> a) a state of well-being and contentment : JOY
>
> b) a pleasurable or satisfying experience

The happiness we'll be building together is a calm, sustainable, positive, warm feeling that forms a backdrop to a successful life. This might also be called contentment or satisfaction.

Happiness, ultimately, is just your brain working at its best. When we feel positive, when we're solution-focused rather than being problem-focused, when our minds and our hearts are open to possibilities, we are at our best. It's the best version of you, ready to encounter anything, likely to make smart decisions, easily able to access your memories, with plenty of available energy, willing to try new things, willing to shed old habits that don't serve you anymore.

So while there will, absolutely, be moments of elation, moments when you're laughing until there are tears flowing down your cheeks, the happiness we're seeking here is a stable state. It's a warm, open-minded, strong, positive approach to anything life might bring.

Attaining this strong, sustained happiness changes everything. The way you tackle problems will change, as will the nature of your relationships. The way you talk to yourself, the way you communicate with others, how much enjoyment you get from your days and the opportunities you're able to pursue will all change. Happiness really is the key to unlocking a remarkable life.

My journey

I went to a prestigious theology college in London. When I'd graduated (with a degree in Philosophy, Religious and Ethics) I was dating my first serious, proper girlfriend and it was time for her to finally meet my family. We got the train down to Plymouth and I introduced her to my mum and my sister. That evening I asked my girlfriend what she thought.

She smiled and said, "You guys talk about your feelings all the time!".

This little remark was a revelation to me. How often do you get an external perspective on your own family? I guess I'd assumed that it was normal for families to talk about emotions, and the nature of the mind, and intrinsic needs, and boundaries, and psycho-social adaptation.

Alongside all the psychology, I also grew up surrounded by hippie ideas. There were crystals, essential oils, copies of the Celestine

Prophesy. I was the cynic of the family, I wanted to rigorously assess everything and throw out ideas that didn't make sense. This lead to some interesting arguments when I was growing up!

As my mum progressed from volunteer for the Samaritans (a phone service for people in psychological distress, often suicidal), to psychotherapist, to University lecturer, I helped her study for her various exams in counselling and psychology. There were always new exams, new books, a new theory. I absorbed so much.

My younger childhood was spent on a farm in Cornwall, and later the little town nearby called Callington. The local primary school was tiny, I could walk there on my own in about 5 minutes. It was a sleepy, safe, cute little Cornish town. I had a close group of friends at school and life was pretty good. I didn't really understand what was happening when my parents got divorced, except that suddenly my dad was up in Scotland for most of the year, running a business that I also didn't really understand. Something to do with risk advice in the North Sea oil industry. He would fly me up to Aberdeen a few times a year and I remember wandering around the town with my day's spending money. To be honest, most of it went to Burger King.

All this changed when I was 11. Dad's business was thriving and there was money to send me to the big public school in Plymouth (in the UK, a fee-paying school with an entrance exam is called a public school). From day 1, I was bullied and ostracised. I was an outsider, the butt of every joke. I was different, and I knew I was different, but as a young teenager that's all I knew. I knew I was failing at most of my classes, I knew I wasn't able to fit in with the cool kids, I knew I was only welcome in the nerd group who were also outcasts.

We moved to Plymouth to be near my new school, but coming from a rural background, I missed having some good soil to grow food, so I got myself an allotment on the edge of the local park. I was growing vegetables when kids my age were going clubbing and learning about drink and weed and sex. I also got into repairing computers and stereos and I did other nerdy stuff. Alex (as everyone called me in those days) became a solemn, sincere, deeply sensitive young man. He couldn't handle criticism or jokes. He took everything seriously, and heard everything as an attack. Other kids seemed to be funnier, quicker, smarter, not so sensitive. They just seemed to get on with things. They didn't wonder why, didn't care about the root truths of things. When the teachers said "you will need to know this for the exam" they wrote it down and went home and read it over and over until they knew it by rote. Alex always seemed to be the first in class to understand things, the first to grasp new ideas, the first to use them in interesting and complex ways that often stumped his teachers. But he would sit down in the exam and not know what to write. His grades were awful.

As an adult, I've had a lot of big conversations with a lot of confused and lost and overwhelmed young people. I've helped them to make sense of things, to join up the dots, to understand why they feel the way they feel. Because how are you meant to join up the dots on your own? Either you get lucky and have people around you who explain things, or you don't care because you just happen to fit in without any need to understand why, or you end up lost and confused. I was the latter.

With the knowledge I have now, what young Alex was going through was this: he had a bit of neurodiversity going on, but not enough to be diagnosed, even with today's diagnostic criteria. Just enough to make his thought processes different to those of his teachers, and his teachers didn't know what ADHD was. Thanks to his upbringing, he knew far too much, far too young, about how minds and emotions work, but he had no idea what to do with this information. He was actively analysing his thoughts and feelings and beliefs, but he was missing all sorts of crucial information that people figure out as they get older. This is where his sensitivity and defensiveness came from. He was failing at school, but too self-aware, too moral and too self-disciplined to be a rebel. It didn't make sense to be a rebel, so he wasn't one. He was a nerd who built computers and played chess. He behaved himself, he followed rules to the letter, and in this trap of knowing too much and understanding too little, he came to an inevitable conclusion, with the kind of certainty that only youth and growing depression can bring.

He clearly and fully came to believe that *he* was the problem. To his sincere, curious, strangely focused mind, he was mentally defective. He was stupid. He hated himself for being so sensitive, so impulsive, such a social reject. Nobody seemed to like him, and he blamed himself for that. He also seemed to feel everything at a very intense pitch, and this made every moment feel overwhelming, and wrong, and hurt so much. As the years at public school went by, he found that all he wanted was to die. Life hurt too much, and he saw so little worth in himself.

For a good 10 years of my life, I was suicidal. As in, actively wishing I could die whenever I wasn't busy or distracted. More people feel like this than you'd realise. You probably know somebody who is actively suicidal but smiles and seems completely fine.

I also had a strong moral code that said that it wasn't ok to cause that much suffering to my family and friends. Suicide absolutely wasn't an option for me. So I was unhappy, and confused, and I searched for answers.

So of course, it became personally essential for me to understand what matters. Why do other people do what they do? Why do other people get out of bed in the morning? How do they decide that life is worth living? I *needed* to know. So I went to study philosophy and theology. As I finished school I was all lined up for a career in IT but I knew I wouldn't survive that. So I went to a tiny, specialist college in London and I studied very hard with priests and ministers and philosophers. People who made their career out of understanding *why*.

University was my salvation, where I learned that I wasn't stupid. My problem was rather the opposite. It wasn't that I was struggling to keep up, and it never had been. Intellect is mostly due to genetics, and I'd got lucky on that front. I understand things fast, I make connections between ideas fast, I can use language to express complex ideas in simple, elegant ways.

My second salvation was falling in love, and getting engaged, and sitting by her bed as she had cancer, and holding her catheter bag as she tottered around the hospital room. I was 23. This rapid journey into adulthood showed me some of the things that people live for. We live for love, for connections with other human beings, for precious things that can (and will) be taken away, so it's very important to embrace them here and now. Being present, noticing what's going on, looking for good in things, became important to me.

Other people do sensible things. They climb career ladders. They save and invest and create personal wealth. They buy property. They vote tactically. They tell little lies in order to negotiate relationships. They stay in challenging or even dead relationships because it seems like a better idea than being alone. None of these things mattered to me, and I fully accept that in a certain way that does make me stupid. For a whole chapter of my life I was in quite a lot of debt.

Instead of mainstream, sensible things, what I've done is obsessively and solemnly chased after meaning, every day, without pause, for the whole of my life. Every book that could show me something, every centre for excellence that I could attend, every person who could teach me. Meditation masters. Sufis and shamans. Philosophers and theologians. Lecturers and researchers. Coaches and therapists.

Tough Thatcherite capitalists and gentle religious leaders. Books on psychology, philosophy, history, mythology. I opened my first business when I was 25, which was a coffee shop, therapy centre and workshop space. At any one time I had at least 20 complementary therapists working for me. Running that business taught me a lot of the missing lessons: marketing, money, staffing, forecasting, how to manage high levels of stress that aren't ever going to go away. It was an intensive education.

I make sure that I'm in the right place to learn the next big lessons. I've been in corporate meetings, I've been on the management group for a big IT team. I've run festivals. I've taken myself where I needed to be to learn the next lessons about what people do, and how, and why.

From Alex to Alexander

The man I am now could not be more different from that solemn, self-destructive boy.

One of my big turning points was when I changed my name from Alex to Alexander.

It was on a hillside in Devon. I was with a tall, imposing, eccentric man called Jonathan, who was the resident shrink at the place I worked. In those days, that place (Embercombe) was a cutting-edge centre for personal and leadership development. People came from around the world to train there. The staff were some of the most impressive people I've ever met. Every day, visitors would arrive in busses and cars to figure out who they are, and how to reach their true selves and their true potential. Inner city kids, ambitious corporate executives on accelerated graduate programmes, lost individuals who were trying to find themselves and their path. It was workshops and it was organic gardening and it was dancing in the kitchen to whatever music someone had brought, and it was conversations that blew your mind every day.

If you worked there, which I did, you were required to see Jonathan. Jonathan was regarded with a bit of awe. For years, my goal as a coach was to be as good as Jonathan. A blend of life experience, intuition, and decades of therapy and coaching lent Jonathan the uncanny ability to say exactly what you needed to hear, exactly when you needed to hear it. I saw him for years, and it was his idea that I become a coach, and he trained me.

'Alex' was the name that others gave me. Short, easy to say, normal, throwaway. A lot of people shorten their names to be more convenient, to make it easier on others. Alex spent most of his life confused, overwhelmed, lost, angry and self-destructive. He had all this passion and intellect and knowledge and potential...but it was chaos. He could barely manage himself and he lurched between jobs, relationships, projects. He actually made a really positive impact in all sorts of ways, but he caused plenty of harm and heartbreak and problems along the way. When I was around 30 years old, things were coming into focus for me. There was now enough clarity to begin putting things in order, to integrate, to come home to the person I was always meant to be.

In one choice, in one moment, I let go of Alex. He was allowed to die which, sadly, was what he always longed for.

Alexander, a very different man, was born. Alexander is robust, focused, determined. Alexander has a clear life path and he's unshakably committed to it. Alexander is stuffed full of learning, and he knows how to use it.

I asked all my friends to start using this new name, and I began introducing myself to people as Alexander. Even many years later, it's still sometimes odd. Yes, I prefer Alexander. I'm asking that you use all those syllables to refer to me. Please take longer to write my name, or to say it.

But I've earned those syllables. I know who I am, and that's a massive achievement.

Where I'm coming from

I've been coaching for a long time now. A good coach, a well-trained coach, has the ability to completely enter the world of a client as they're speaking. My core identity remains unchanged, but for an hour, I am visiting my client's life and seeing things through their eyes. I bring my knowledge and expertise to them, and like Jonathan used to do for me, I say exactly what they need to hear, exactly when they need to hear it. As they walk out the room, I come back to my life and remember what it's like to be me. These days the life that I come back to is a good life. I love my life. I am a profoundly happy man, and I say that as somebody who was unhappy for a long time. I had to earn my happiness, I had to understand all its rules and criteria. I had to learn, consciously, to navigate the challenges of life because I was so very bad at just following along.

So I know about happiness, and love, and meaning. And I know about money, and business, and success. I know about analysis and problem-solving, and how to build habits that make big personal problems go away. I know about life, and death, and belonging, and suffering, and relating, and all of the ways in which a human being can thrive. And I know about making sense of things. I am happy, and financially successful, and I have great connections, and I'm proud of what I've achieved.

I've visited hundreds of lives. In our time together, my clients lend me a kind of vulnerability and trust that they will offer few others in their lives, and I see, truly, what's going on. People walk into my clinic, or log on to their online coaching calls, with trepidation and excitement. I am their advisor, their guide and their companion. Through them, I have learned so much. We find robust, practical solutions together, and I've tested them in hundreds of situations, and worked out what makes sense and what doesn't.

And that is what this short series of books is about. It's lessons I learned from the books about psychology and philosophy and neuro-science. It's the core truths I teased from meditation experts and mystics and economists and therapists. It's the solutions I developed with my clients. It's my own conclusions about how ancient myths morphed into modern stories that continue to tell us profound things about ourselves. It's a blend of theory and practice. It's all of this, offered with nothing but the hope that your life will be enriched, enhanced and improved.

Most authors have one single idea that they want to convey, and writing a book is mostly about padding out that idea to fill pages. If you've read personal development books before, you know what I mean. You can often read the first couple of chapters, then read the conclusion, and you get most of the value from the book.

These 3 books aren't like that.

I encourage you to read this series from beginning to end, rather than jump from place to place. Once you've read the whole series, feel free to dip back into the parts that feel most helpful for you.

Masks: the first barrier to progress

As it turns out, people can go their whole lives without ever really knowing who they really are. People can have decades-long marriages and never truly meet one another. This is because most people are wearing masks, most of the time.

'Masks' are the artificial selves we construct in order to fit in. We learn the first ones early in life. Perhaps you were too noisy or energised and your parents shouted at you to be quiet all the time…so you learned the mask of being a quiet and docile person. Perhaps your father didn't know how to handle stress and would explode when things happened at home, and perhaps you adopted his mask.

From there, we keep learning masks. If a job is a hostile place, we might learn a mask of conformity, or playing the joker, or over-performing in order to feel safe. Women often learn the mask of being agreeable and pleasant to men, because it protects them from hostility. Men, conversely, often learn a mask of being over-masculine because they believe their vulnerability will be seen as a weakness. A new role might require that you pretend to be more confident than you feel, and you wear the mask that projects this confidence, even though that's not how you feel inside.

We control our facial expressions, we're carefully about what we say, we hold our bodies in certain ways, we shift our tone of voice. We want to appear in certain ways when we're in certain places or with certain people. It can be a smart social adaptation, but it can also become a prison.

What matters most to you about the way other people see you? Perhaps you want to seem happy, or in control, or highly skilled, or likeable, or impressive, or attractive, or like you know what you're doing? These will tell you what kinds of masks you're likely to wear.

Masks are essential for social functioning – it makes a lot of sense to shield yourself from people you can't trust, and in a lot of situations you don't want to be 100% real and vulnerable. In the middle of a board meeting, you don't want to burst out crying. A doctor can't afford to seem uncertain when giving advice to a patient. A parent wants their children to feel safe, so they project calm and confidence when they don't feel it.

Masks can be conscious or unconscious. They are conscious when we *know* we're putting effort into shaping our appearance, our words, our choices and our behaviour to suit others. We smile at our children even when we've had a hard day. We tell our boss we're on top of something that's overwhelming us. We log on to a work call sounding positive and up-beat, even if we feel crappy. We tell our friends that everything's fine at home even when it's not.

For some people, wearing conscious masks are the norm, they're fine, they're just part of life. As they arrive at work they consciously put their mask in place and that's something they feel absolutely comfortable with. For other people, it's uncomfortable or tiring to wear them and they look forward to being able to take them off in the privacy of their home, or with their best friends, or with their partner.

If you're choosing to wear a mask, that's fine from a personal development perspective. That's not going to get in the way of your personal growth.

Unconscious masks, however, are where the first major barrier to personal development comes in. For many people this will be the main problem that stops them creating lasting happiness in their lives.

Unconscious masks never (or almost never) come off. Early-life lessons or traumatic experiences have taught us to always wear a mask, from the moment we wake to the moment we go to sleep. Perhaps we should always be pleasant. Perhaps we should always seem happy. Perhaps we should always be looking after others. Or perhaps we wear a mask of power, dominance or control. We don't even notice, most of the time, that we're wearing these masks and even as we become more conscious of them it's incredibly hard to stop reverting back to them in certain situations. Maybe we learn to take our masks off, because we want to express ourselves more authentically in more situations. But time passes and then we notice that we've put the mask back on. Maybe at work, or with new people, or when intimidated, or when visiting our parents.

To me, and to anyone who is serious about personal development, unconscious masks are a huge problem. They stop us properly accessing our feelings, beliefs, impulses and true responses to things. If we're wearing masks all the time then when we try to understand ourselves and begin making positive changes, what we're really doing is trying to develop our masks. Only when we drop our masks entirely and stand naked, raw and authentic can we meet our real selves. Without this experience of a true self, it's incredibly hard to make headway in growing towards happiness and satisfaction.

I am lucky enough to be trained to see through masks, both the conscious type and the unconscious type. It's a large part of my work. So I move through my day seeing the real people underneath the masks they project in the world.

Most often, what I see behind people's masks is this:

A fear that somebody will notice how much we're secretly struggling. Confusion on so many levels, and the hope that things will work out but no real sense of being in control. A lack of knowing who we really are and what will most deeply satisfy us. Not knowing how to identify, under-stand or safely express emotions. Unsatisfied needs of all kinds, which aren't acknowledged or understood, which cause erratic and self-sabotaging behaviour. Because of this, a lack of trust in ourselves. The search for belong-ing, and connection, and identity, and safety, and pride, and contentment...but without any idea about how to engage in this search, or even that the search is important. Ultimately: struggle; fear; desperation; dissatisfaction.

That, I believe, is just how most people move through life, and they keep themselves so busy so they don't have time to notice or acknowledge how hard and out-of-control life feels.

This inner turbulence leads to patterns of choices, and ways of communicating, and spur-of-the-moment decisions, that add up into predictable results. When this chaos and dissatisfaction exists inside us, it manifests as unsatisfying relationships and friendships, or the unhealthy use of drink and drugs, or trouble with money, or bad relationships with the body, or bad parenting, or stifled and unsatisfying careers, or trouble expressing ourselves, or difficulties setting clear goals and following through.

It is the person behind the masks who needs to grow and develop. I don't want to help you develop a better mask to cover over the things that you try to hide. This trilogy is about much deeper trans-formation than that. We want to replace confusion with control, to replace fear or insecurity with robust self-knowledge, to replace any sense of longing or needing with the confidence that all your fundamental needs are being satisfied by the kind of life you're living.

To make progress like this, we need to be able to access our true feelings, thoughts, beliefs and wounds, which are all hidden under the masks we wear. If you can't access those, your personal devel-opment will just amount to crafting better masks, and you'll never find true happiness because you will never really be present in the moments of your life.

So at this point, I'd encourage you to begin noticing the shapes of your masks. Do you know what masks you wear? Do you know your conscious masks and your unconscious masks? Do you know what you are presenting to the world, which isn't really the authentic you?

You don't need to figure this all out at once, and I'm not asking you to throw your masks away just yet. The important thing is to become conscious of the things you do every day which feel authentic, and the things you do which are masks you wear to protect yourself or to be accepted.

Examples of masks people wear

- The tough survivor, who never lets anyone see their true feelings.
- A mask of confident leadership which someone might wear to hide their fears. Perhaps a fear of failing, a fear of not being able to perform or a sense of imposter-syndrome.
- The victim, who talks all the time about how life is so hard and looks for people to help them all the time.
- The rescuer, who looks for victims to rescue and shows everyone how virtuous they are by helping everyone.
- The persecutor or bully, who masks their own insecurities by attacking others.
- The over-performer or over-achiever, which might mean: the perfect daughter or son, the perfect husband or wife, the one who always seeks to impress their boss. The consistent thing is the pressure they put on themselves to always seem perfect or impressive.
- The joker, who distracts everyone from seeing who they really are by making everyone laugh all the time.
- The docile or compliant woman who doesn't trigger men.

- The manly man, which means a man who feels they need to amplify certain traits, or use a certain tone of voice, or only express certain views, in order to feel masculine enough.

Arete

I'll be using this word a lot, so I'll begin with a definition, and then I'll explain why it's so important.

Arete

Greek

NOUN

excellence or *virtue, esp. in the full* realization of *potential* or *inherent* function by a person or thing

Webster's New World College Dictionary

In ancient times, Greek philosophers were working on first principles. They weren't drawing on centuries of science and tradition, they were trying to figure stuff out for the first time. That's part of the reason we continue to read their words today: sometimes it helps to go back to the beginning and start to work things out from there.

These philosophers were living at the dawn of Western democracy, so it was important for them to figure out the answers to important questions. For example, ethics. What is right and wrong? How do you know? Do you adhere to your own rules, and does it even matter if you do?

One of the core ideas they were exploring was this word: *Arete*. There are various ideas about how to pronounce it, but I go with ar-ret-tay.

In practice, when philosophers like Aristotle were using the word *Arete* they meant excellence, or virtue, or the highest or best version of something.

We behave with *Arete* when we manifest the best version of ourselves. We work with *Arete* if we are working with the intention to deliver excellence. We pursue *Arete* in our relationships when we try to show up as the best version of ourselves for our partner, and work over time to make the relationship the best and most fulfilling it can possibly be. We can bring *Arete* to our parenting, our hobbies, our exercise, our friendships, or adventures and the kind of home we make for ourselves.

Ultimately, we ourselves can become *Arete* when we decide to let excellence be our guiding principle, and consistently work over time to become the highest, best version of ourselves.

The idea is not that we're trying to measure up to some outside idea from someone else, but that we're pursuing the best that we can achieve, judged by our own ideas of whatever the highest version of something might be. We're not settling for just anything. We're interested in excellence, in finding out what excellence means for us and then chasing after it.

I want to help you get the most out of your life, and I want to help you become the happiest, wisest, most successful, best version of yourself. Your own personal *Arete*. I'm not interested in imposing my ideas of what this looks like for you, or anyone else's template of who and what you should be. You might immediately be imagining what 'excellence' looks like, and that can easily become a burden or a straight jacket because we're trying to live up to this image. But you can't know, yet, what *Arete* will look like for you. You will discover that as you go. It won't conform to anyone else's ideas or who they believe you should be.

The core idea here is simply that excellence matters, that settling for ok is not ok, and people who attain lasting happiness will also have this idea of *Arete*, whether they call it that or not, and be working to unlock the highest and best version of themselves. This book is written with this belief in mind.

To my way of thinking, why would you not try to reach your maximum potential? Why would you settle for anything less?

Happiness is the goal of this series, and as you take steps towards your best self you're going to discover more of this background sense of ease, peace, satisfaction and positivity.

As you get closer and closer to your own personal *Arete*, you'll find that masks cease to be useful to you. You're going to know your vulnerabilities, your flaws, your trigger points, your psychological wounds and how they are expressed in feelings, words and choices. You will own them, be familiar with them and where they come from, and be working to heal the parts of you that feel they need a mask in order to be safe. You will have the wisdom and the strength to be ok with who you are, and so you'll have nothing to hide or to avoid. You will know your limitations and foibles and you'll be ok with them. You will be intensely comfortable in your own skin, and committed to the life you have created.

Some things help to achieve this. Certain knowledge, certain language, certain types of choices. I'll be providing those things in this book. Alongside these, there are plenty of things that seem like they'll help, but which are actually distracting or counter-productive. I'll be trying to flag those up too.

Arete people stand out

You might know some people who embody *Arete*, or who are obviously pursuing excellence in their lives. They stand out. They tend to have considered things thoroughly and have interesting opinions and insights. They have plans and ideas about the future. They're very clear about what's important in life. Often, they are doing things with their lives that help others. They possess a kind of grounded confidence and charisma, which isn't showy or attention-grabbing. They have no need to control, coerce or manipulate anyone. They are merely sure of themselves, and moving through their lives with purpose and focus.

If you've known one of these people, or if you have perhaps been working towards *Arete* for a while, you know how unusual these people feel. They tend to feel more solid than other people. Trustworthy. Real. Potent.

That's not to say that *Arete* people are superhuman, or never get upset or overwhelmed, never make mistakes, never experience confusion or doubt, never have personal crises. However, they do have the self-knowledge and the skills to handle these things, and they have a strong framework to put every challenge into context. They are robust, resilient and adaptable because of the knowledge they've found on their journey.

So this work *is worth* it. There is a kind of joy that can only be known by those who have embarked on a journey to find themselves and their manifestation of *Arete*. A feeling of fierce and powerful aliveness and presence, a certainty of purpose, a deep joy and a series of heartfelt connections with other people, with the place where we belong, with the purpose to which we feel called and to which we have dedicated out lives. A freedom, a focus, a sense of being awake and aware. The relaxation and calm that comes from being only who we truly are. Delight from simple things.

How do we reach *Arete*?

Attaining *Arete* is the point of the 12 Rules in the next book. In this book, we're equipping ourselves with the building blocks and toolkit for making that journey.

However, the journey begins when we find the courage to peer under the masks that we wear every day, and honestly take a look at the person who lies underneath. There will be things you've avoided looking at, things you don't like, but there will also be your genius, your unique strengths, the skills you've mastered…

Throughout the rest of this book I'll be talking about exploring this 'true self'. Try, wherever possible, to distinguish this self from the masks you've grown used to wearing. You have the power to shed your masks. You created them, and some part of you continues to wear them, but they are not prisons from which you cannot escape. With enough time and enough understanding, you can put aside any masks that don't support your journey towards your personal *Arete*.

Three paths, one journey

As you'll have noticed, I tend to talk about personal development as a 'journey'. Everyone seems to start using this word as they work on themselves, as the scale of the work becomes apparent. Perhaps it sounds a bit corny, but it's absolutely how it feels as you learn, realise things about your personality, feelings, beliefs and choices, and as things begin to join up and make more sense.

On this journey, it can be helpful to break life into three aspects: being; doing; and relating. Sometimes you'll be focused on one of these 'paths' more than the others, but they all need attention, and there's always something new to learn for each. So many of my clients tell me how much easier this would be if they could just put two paths on hold while they focus on one of them: growing their career; improving relations with their family; rediscovering intimacy in their relationship; focusing on their parenting or taking time out to simply be with themselves without all the pressures of their lives.

Unfortunately, it doesn't really work like that. Each depends upon the other, and you will go further, faster, by accepting that you need to walk all three at once.

The path of **Being** is the path of your relationship with yourself. It is your inner work, your psycho-spiritual, physical and emotional development. It is coming to know yourself deeply and feeling comfortable with your own strengths, foibles and eccentricities. It is being at home in your own skin.

The path of **Doing** is your outer effects in the world. This means the impact you have, the difference you make, the kind of work you're doing and what you choose to do with your time. It includes your career, your home, your hobbies and activities.

The path of **Relating** is about how you interact with other people. How do you relate to friends, family, lovers, partners, colleagues and strangers? Are you balanced and fair or do you tend to emphasise their needs or yours? Do you tend to get what you want out of relationships? Are you bringing your mature, empowered self to relationships or do you tend to bring a more infantile version of yourself? Do you risk having disruptive, important conversations with a partner, or do you feel safer letting things tick along, even at the risk of things getting stale?

Focusing on just one of these paths and ignoring the others will significantly stifle your growth. As much as we might want to put our career on hold to work on ourselves, our inner work cannot be completed without an outer world to relate to. To grow as a person but not in relationships will leave you lonely, or unseen, or unsatisfied, or build relationships that are fractured and underwhelming. To make strides in your work life but not in your inner development will risk finding yourself financially fulfilled but emotionally hollow. I've worked with many millionaire clients who are profoundly miserable. We have to keep the balance.

The paths reinforce one another. Nothing in life is harder than deeply relating to another human being with a mature balance of vulnerability and clear boundaries, but developing these skills with your partner will see you finding new ways to deal with conflict or communication at work. Your job will be significantly different if you bring an emotionally resolved, empowered, healthily ambitious version of yourself to it. Beautiful and interesting things happen when the three trails of our lives touch one another, and we notice a cross-over in our personal growth.

So, as you walk this journey, be aware of the three paths that you are treading. What is most important for you, right now? Are the paths closely aligned with one another, going in the same direction, or are they pulling you apart? Which are you most committed to right now? Where do you need to grow, develop and change? Have you neglected things that need your attention? This awareness will serve you through this book and through your own personal journey, and I'll be talking about the three paths as we start to develop the themes of this series.

Life in a prison: the domesticated human

Why do smart people end up in unhappy lives? Why is it that so many of us feel trapped in a life that just isn't meeting our needs?

I've watched hundreds of lives change, and I know that everyone's life can be a positive, exciting adventure full of prosperity and success. We can each feel calm in ourselves, confident, in control, and ready to greet whatever the day brings.

But an unsatisfying life can feel like a prison cell. We look at other people living happier, better lives, and it can be easy to believe we'll never have what they have, never be so happy, content or successful.

So many of us spend years living lives that feel sad, frustrating, and uninspired. But why?

My coaching is all about finding freedom and happiness by asking deep, probing questions that take us into difficult places. From there, we find the knowledge and strategies we need to reshape our lives. When it comes to understanding the prison that keeps so many of us trapped, the key questions are: what's forcing us to live these unsatisfying lives; and what should we be doing to change our situation?

There are always practical reasons to stay where we are...

- This job may not nourish my soul, but it's good enough, and I can't afford to make changes right now.
- My friends don't really get me, but it's better than not having friends.
- My relationship hasn't felt exciting or passionate for years, but it's nice to have someone to come home to and besides, we have a home together and disentangling things could be messy, painful and expensive.
- I could start a training course or head in a new direction in my life, but I don't really know what I want to do and I wouldn't know what to choose.

Often our emotions are a big part of this. We can be afraid of all sorts of things. Being unable to provide for ourselves or our families. Being alone. Doing things that seem too big or frightening to handle. Being afraid of ourselves and what we might find if we dig too deep, or if we let go of all the strategies that we're currently using.

We're mammals, and other than our very big brains, we're very similar to other mammals in most ways. Our nervous systems are wired in similar ways, and a whole section of our brain is often called the 'mammalian brain' because it works exactly like the brain of an ape, or a dog, or a horse. While we're very clever in all sorts of ways, so many of our responses, feelings and other things that contribute to our decision-making are animalistic. We're going to be teasing apart our animal and human selves in this series, because a happy life is one that keeps the animal-self happy *and* meets the complex needs of the human being.

So I want to begin by talking about other mammals, because they can give us clues about what's going on in human animals.

Imagine you're visiting a farm. You see cows and sheep gently grazing in the fields. Are they energetic and rushing around or do they plod from place to place with nowhere to go? I grew up on a farm, and all the animals were basically placid and content with their situation. If a gate is left open, the animals might wander out, but this is less a desperate bid for escape and more the plodding meander of an animal looking for food. They're calm, docile creatures. They're also dependent on us. They wouldn't survive for very long without the humans who bring them food, or tend to their medical needs, or keep them safe from predators. Some of our farm animals have become so dependent on us that they will quickly die without human support.

We've bred these animals over time to make them dependent and docile. They have no idea that their lives exist to feed the people they depend on. They just chew the grass and accept that this is the way things are. This is domestication.

Wild animals are different from their domesticated cousins. A wild animal is more alert, more curious and more aware of its surroundings. It has to be: food might be scarce, and it might need to hunt around for food. Predators could wait in the shadows or around the next corner. Death is a constant companion, never very far away. A wild animal is wary, cautious and forced to explore and experiment. Its senses are sharper and its mind more alert. It lives on the edge between life and death and it makes no assumptions about how tomorrow might be.

A wild animal will also tend to be more sociable, especially higher mammals like horses, wolves, elephants or dolphins. They will play, compete, mate, travel, hunt and scrap in ways that you won't see so often in a field of sleepy cattle. In some species there are leaders that make the decisions. Relationships are strong and animals will recognise each other and pick up their relationships after being separated. Wild animals display emotions more obviously and more freely than their docile counterparts. The social structures in wild herds, packs or pods exist in part to stop this wildness, this freedom, from running out of control.

How do we measure the difference between a wild animal and its domesticated counterparts? Researchers will often refer to how much an animal will tolerate being contained in a small space. Many wild animals can't bear being confined in small spaces. A wild animal in a trap will often hurt itself or even kill itself in its desperation to escape. It needs freedom, it needs space to run, fly, forage and nest. When locked into a small space with others of its kind it has a much lower tolerance for being pressed-up against other animals.

Compare this to a herd of cattle, who will stand patiently in a pen with dozens of other cows, pressed up against each other, their only objection being a bit of mooing. Put only a couple of wild horses into the same pen and they'll become stressed and anxious, lashing out to break free.

Just the way things are

Humans are the only species that have domesticated themselves. We've trained ourselves and our children to be calm and ok with feeling trapped. Have you ever had a hard day and you just wanted to shout or scream or smash something, but of course you were at work, or with family or in a public place so you just had to hold it in? Have you ever been in a bustling crowd and just wanted to be somewhere else so you can breathe? Even people I meet who are really, desperately fed up with their lives don't actually spend that much of the day thinking about it. We're too busy. We have jobs to do, kids to feed, bills to pay, complicated lives to organise. We have tv shows to watch, friends to hang out with, people to take care of, social media to scroll through. We simply don't have time to reflect too much on the things that are hard.

Just like other domesticated animals, we've become dependent on the systems that keep us alive. We go to work so we'll have the money to buy things, pay our mortgage and provide for ourselves. We buy our food pre-prepared in shops, our wealth is managed by banks, our conversations are often electronic, our medicines are issues by doctors and the way we raise our children is directed by tradition and by the school system.

Somewhere, hidden in this life of comfort and dependence, is the true nature of the prison that stops us breaking free and building more nourishing lives for ourselves.

The thing that keeps us stuck and trapped is an attitude. I call it: 'just the way things are'.

This is the attitude that most people use, most of the time. You might feel that you hate your job. But doesn't everyone? Always panicked about money or trying to make it from one payslip to another? That's normal, isn't it? Sex is boring or rare? That's just the way things are, right? Feel too shy to speak your truth? Working long, exhausting hours? Enduring fights or persecution at home? That's just the way things are.

In the end, our domesticated minds will turn anything into 'just the way things are'. It's this human ability to normalise hurtful things that has caused the most suffering in history. It's happening right now. Every day we endure lives that aren't right for us, that don't bring us the full measure of joy and wonder that is our birth-right. We accept this because we've normalised it. In the same way, we might walk past homeless people every day, or we buy products that we know were made by people who are suffering, or we hear the droning of politicians that clearly worsens the suffering of vulnerable people, and we shrug it off.

In psychology, we refer to the "comfort zone" as being the parts of our lives that feel familiar,normal and safe. This includes things like your home, close relationships, work, and habits. We become used to our comfort zones. As we'll explore later in this series, we need to be very careful about our choices, because domesticated humans will always choose comfort over happiness. The longer we stay in this safe bubble, the less we can see anything outside. All we see is the way things are right now. We lose sight of the huge range of possibilities, options, experiences, feelings, ideas and sensations that also exist out beyond the limits of what we know.

'Just the way things are' begins early in life. Unless we were incredibly lucky, our parents lived the same way. If we confronted them with questions that challenge their own 'just the way things are', as all children do, our parents tended not to know how to handle them. Maybe they distracted us, maybe they gave us the only answers they knew, or maybe they shamed us into silence. As adults, they had learned to stop asking deep questions of themselves.

School does its part in teaching you 'just the way things are'. By school age, you're expected to have stopped asking a lot of the inconvenient questions, and you'll be given good marks for playing by the rules, memorising facts and reproducing them in the right ways. None of this is done maliciously: for the teachers this is also 'just the way things are'. They provide the learning and guidance to show us how things are, and we enthusiastically join in, enforcing rules and social structures, resorting to bullying and mocking anyone who stands out, has unusual ideas, or still has a wild, curious edge. You might have been one of the people who failed to learn the rules quickly enough, or you might have been one of those who enforced the social norms. Either way, you learned 'just the way things are' sooner or later. Embarrassment, shame and social exclusion are usually the punishments for not fitting in.

For most of the rest of our lives, we can have this feeling of being weirdos or outsiders if we continue to ask questions. The French philosopher Albert Camus wrote the book *The Outsider* all about this feeling of not fitting in with the template that society expects of us.

People around us seem to be ok with the way things are, and it doesn't occur to them to wonder if they could be otherwise. Often what's going on under the surface for these people is that they also feel uncomfortable and trapped, but their anger and urge to change has turned inwards, becoming bitterness and resentment towards those who continue to ask, to challenge, to try to find a better life.

So, from within and without, we are encouraged to believe that this is all there is. Maybe you can imagine another life, but it's just a dream. It's just fantasy. Here and now is what's real. We tend to feel free, but this learning goes deep, far deeper than just deciding what to do with our day. It tells us, in subtle ways that we hardly ever notice, how to think, how to feel, what to believe in, what to trust, things that are good and things that are bad.

That's the prison. Anyone in this prison who feels trapped, overwhelmed, disappointed or frustrated has the ability to break free. What holds us back is a deeply ingrained belief that things cannot change. That even trying to change certain things is wrong or pointless.

In this series I'll be asking you questions and inviting you to consider things from new perspectives. But more than anything else, this book is about restoring the power that is rightfully yours. Nothing can stop you if you are focused and determined. Whatever it is that you want, you can have, if you are willing to step forward and do the inner and outer work to make it happen.

What if everything could change? What if your thoughts could change? What if the emotions you feel could be different? What if the way you talk to people and the way they treat you could change? What if you could be doing radically different work that makes you feel good? What if you could connect to people in new ways, transforming your friendships and your relationships? What if sex could be better and more fulfilling than you ever knew? What if you could feel like you're a positive force in the world, that you're part of something significant and important?

What if you could rediscover yourself as a free, wild animal?

If you spend time with successful entrepreneurs, or successful artists, or community leaders, or indeed anybody who stands out as strong, creative and open-minded, you'll find an entirely different attitude to 'just the way things are'. You'll find a person who has rediscovered much of their wild nature, a person who doesn't allow things to become normal, a person who is always curious, always learning.

I'll be talking a lot about choices in this series. It's been my experience that, on some level, we make choices that either empower and free us, or which keep us safe but stifled. It's our choices, from the very small to the very large, that define the shape of our lives. At this point, you don't need to know how to fully embrace this power, or what to do with it, or even what it really means. At the beginning of your journey, I just want to invite you to allow the possibility that if you ever feel trapped, stuck, squashed, frustrated, or unsatisfied, it's because on some level you've chosen to let that happen to you. It doesn't mean there's anything wrong with you, it's very normal in this culture. But it's not the only way to live. As we'll explore later in this book, power and responsibility go hand-in-hand. You cannot truly have one without the other. If you want to shake up your life and break through into a new way of feeling, being and living, then it begins with looking at the life you have now and saying:

"My choices brought me here, and as long as I continue to choose the things I've always chosen, my life will continue to look the same way."

Without strength, nothing else is possible

Life is messy. Whatever else life is, however we choose to look at it, and whatever personal lessons we've learned along the way, life is messy. It is chaos and churn and complexity and a constant juggling act. Whatever shape your life has, it will be a struggle at times.

Buddhism and I have a bad history. We don't get along. I've trained in lots of spiritual disciplines, from Catholicism to whirling with Sufis. Each tradition looks at the challenges of being alive and looks for answers to our deepest questions, filtered through their own belief structures. I deeply respect a lot of the things that Buddhist traditions have discovered about the human condition (we wouldn't have modern Mindfulness without thousands of years of Buddhist research) but I do not like their conclusions.

At the heart of Buddhism is the idea that suffering comes from attachment, and therefore severing our attachments to the world will free us from suffering. Yes, that makes logical sense, but I take a completely different approach and belief.

I much prefer shamanic and indigenous spirituality. Here, suffering is an ally. We do not seek to escape it, we seek to be strong enough to transmute it into something else. We take pride in our strength and our forbearance and our ability to thrive in spite of the struggles.

I think this is really important for everything we might want to do in our lives. Strength is necessary for anything else we might want...

- The strength to have difficult, essential conversations
- The strength to keep moving, even when we feel weak, emotional or overwhelmed
- The strength to face important things about ourselves, our lives, our family or our relationships
- The strength to change and grow
- The strength to leave our comfort zone

So an essential part of our work is to understand and develop our strength. But what does it really mean to be mentally and emotionally strong? How do we become stronger?

How do we remain centred and focused, even as things get harder around us? Can we develop ourselves into something formidable, something unstoppable, somebody so strong that we can achieve anything that we desire, no matter how hard?

What samurai can teach us about strength

Japanese martial arts have been a cornerstone of my life. They involve a lot of sweating, shouting, being punched, performing kata as perfectly as you can, holding yourself in difficult poses as your muscles shake, sometimes some bleeding, often pushing yourself to your absolute limits.

While you're developing your physical power and endurance, you're also developing mentally and spiritually. You're reading the philosophy and guiding principles of martial arts masters. Your sensei is posing questions and challenging you to consider how you will use the power you now have. A bully or a recklessly violent person will often lash out because they know they are weak and they're trying to prove something or dominate a situation. As you notice yourself become more dangerous, it becomes personally relevant to consider how you'll behave. You are steered away from any notions that you can use your new power to do random violence, and you're encouraged to think virtuously and with moral responsibility.

There's a lot of reference to a samurai mindset, which goes something like this: at my side is a sword, and if I draw my sword then I am utterly lethal. I train every day to be more and more lethal. I am quite capable of breaking someone down, of crushing them, of using my skill and strength to hurt them or even kill them. I can take a life, in violence and savagery. This is not theory or an idea from a book, this is a reality I live every day.

But I don't, and I absolutely will not unless I have exhausted every other option. I am absolutely beholden to keep my sword sheathed and my violence in check. I must always try to avoid drawing my sword: I must walk away from situations, run if I have to, or try to defuse violence with words. Only when all other options have been explored will I resort to violence. There are very strict moral guidelines around when it's ok to use violence (for example, defending a vulnerable person from violence). If I ever do reach this point I will deploy every shred of my skill to end the situation as quickly as possible.

It's this forbearance that's part of my understanding of true strength.

One day in my 20s, I was putting up some signs in the window of my business. It was a normal day, in a normal week. One of my staff was holding the ladder I was standing on. Then suddenly she says "what is that man doing to that woman?"

I frown and look down at her. I see where she's looking and follow her gaze. At the end of the street, at a bus stop, a man has hold of a woman by her hair and he is slamming her head repeatedly into a railing while shouting at her. Other people are standing at the bus stop, doing nothing, looking in any direction except at the violence unfolding right beside them. The moment is surreal and I can't really believe it's happening, and it takes me (to my shame) a little while to climb down off the ladder and walk over to them. I remember walking up that cobbled street as if I was watching myself from the outside, trying to work out if I was dreaming or something, it all seemed such a sudden departure from the utterly normal day I had been living only seconds before.

I eventually reach them. I don't know what to do. He's let go of her and he turns to face me. He shouts at me, but I'm more interested in how she's doing. She seems to be scared, and not making eye contact with anyone, but not actually badly injured. He keeps shouting at me and when I gently tell him to calm down, he hits my chest.

I have many years of martial arts training by this point. Every morning I train for an hour with a formidable, ex-military teacher who has extreme skill and strength. So as this man hits me, my centre of gravity is low. My muscles are well developed, and I am used to being hit. He bounces off me. I don't move at all.

I begin, in this surreal moment, to wonder if I will need to hit this man. Is this going to be my first real fight? Then, to complete the unreality of the moment, the woman asks me to leave. Harder than this man's attempt to hurt me, it hits me that I might be actually making her life more dangerous by intervening. I have no idea what to do. The man and the woman go to stand together at the bus stop, waiting along with everyone else. They fade back into being just regular folk, living regular lives, waiting for a bus.

Nobody else has reacted at all. I walk away.

While there's a lot to unpack there, and perhaps you would have handled it differently, I am proud of the strength I had in that situation. Where others avoided or ignored, I challenged. Where I could have lashed out, through emotion or ignorance, I was patient. Where a force of true derangement and toxicity tried to hurt me, I was unmoved. I did what I believed was right and I wasn't paralysed, overwhelmed or reckless.

I think I embodied strength in that encounter.

The three tiers of strength

So I'm going to share with you how I believe strength works. While we're going to feel stronger or weaker at different moments, we can develop our baseline level of personal strength. This idea of developing strength is woven in to the 12 Rules of *Arete*. We can grow and become stronger over time.

There are three stages in strength…

The first tier: lacking strength

We are all weak sometimes.

In this state, life hits us hard. Things feel very difficult and we can struggle to be effective at the things that matter to us.

We can get stuck in an unhappy situation for hours, days, even years.

We can lose faith in ourselves.

We can struggle to communicate well, losing our words or failing to be heard in conversations and situations where we really want to be understood.

Our fears, doubts, neuroses and insecurities win sometimes. All we hear is the voice of our inner critic, or our emotions wash over us and take away our agency, our ability to act.

Have you ever been here? Have you felt what this is like? Do you know others who have?

We all end up here at some point, and actually I believe that knowing this place is essential for personal development. People who have never felt this state never really understand what's at stake. They miss something essential about what life is about. Feeling weak is an important foundation piece to a person's life.

However, it is not the end of the story. It is never the end of the story. For everyone, there is always a route to strength. We might begin with the smallest victories, but beginning to move is essential, as is the belief, even if it's very small, that unlocking personal strength is possible.

We might all be weak sometimes, but we all have the capacity and the potential to grow into strong, formidable, resilient people. Achieving this is a matter of knowledge, understanding and focused willpower. Throughout this trilogy of books, I will share all three of these things with you.

The second tier: toughness

What I mean by 'toughness' is what a lot of people consider to be personal strength. It's a common misconception. It means:

Not feeling things, or pretending you don't, or acting like you don't.

The goal, for many people, is to be closed-off or numb to the world. The belief goes that by doing this we are being the strongest we can be. You'll see this in men who act tough and women who try not to let anything bother them. We all know these people.

It's a totally understandable goal. If you've been paralysed or overwhelmed in the past, or if you've seen people who are, then it makes sense that the opposite of that is to be unaffected by feelings, or challenges, or other people. It makes sense to close down, or move through life too quickly to get pinned down and threatened, or to push away anything or anyone who gets too close.

But at the root of this behaviour and this belief is fear. Behaviour that seems strong and tough and invulnerable, is actually a declaration of insecurity. You are saying, to those who understand these things, that you don't believe in yourself, that you know that if you stopped to feel things, or noticed what your body or intuition is telling you, or if you lowered your defences, you would lose yourself. It is, in effect, simple running-away. It's trying to escape from life by wrapping yourself in a defensive barrier. This is not true strength.

Vulgar displays of power

Another misconception is that being violent is being strong. This violence could be physical, but more often it shows up as:

- Emotional violence – being callous or unkind to people, because you believe it makes you seem strong

- Social dominance – mocking people, attacking differences in beliefs or lifestyle, being a bully. Again, this is the idea that we are strong because we can put others down

- Prejudice and hostility based on arbitrary things like skin colour, sexual orientation or gender

Again, these kinds of behaviour announce to people who understand the nature of personal strength, that you are afraid and insecure. People who behave like this are trying to create the illusion of strength by preying on the weakness of others. If I attack you, or undermine you, or mock you, or gaslight you, I make you feel weak and vulnerable so by comparison I look stronger. This is another way to say, I doubt my own strength and I need to undermine others so my own insecurity isn't noticed by anyone else.

The third tier: true strength

Personal strength is knowing yourself very well, understanding who you are and what makes you tick, having effective strategies to manage your trigger-points and neuroses, and finding a deep trust that you can manage yourself.

One of the highest states that a person in our culture can achieve is the heartfelt feelings of "I'm ok". That's it. It sounds so easy, it sounds so simple. And yet how many of us can say that truly feel ok with ourselves? How many of us feel like we trust ourselves, trust how we'll handle any situation, trust our emotions, trust our life strategies?

In my experience, this kind of peace is the end of a long road of enquiry, fear, making mistakes, learning and adapting and finally accepting the deep truth of who you are. It is a hard-won state which I see very rarely in people.

It is true strength. A person who occupies this place will:

- Regularly ask for help, without a moment's worry that asking for help is wrong.

- Be emotionally vulnerable with the people who matter, letting them see everything, without any fear that this level of vulnerability will threaten them.

- Admit when they don't know, or don't understand, because looking foolish isn't a problem.

- Intentionally leave their comfort zone on a regular basis, knowing they will make mistakes, because learning and growing is important.

- Laugh often, because joy is it's own goal and they don't care that people might not appreciate their happiness.

- Love passionately, not holding back through fear of it all going wrong, because they know what loss and heartbreak are like, and they trust themselves not to be unmade by it.

- Maintain clear and honest boundaries, that don't shift, because keeping themselves psychologically and physically safe is very important and their own well-being is more important than pleasing others.

- Be engaged with ongoing personal growth, because as much as we learn to trust ourselves we also know that there is always stuff to work on.

So here I might be flipping some people's idea of strength on its head. So many cultural stories tell us that a strong person is impervious, unmoved, unchanging. Movies and books sell us characters who are like this, and we're meant to believe that they're the strong ones. But they're not. They are rigid, they're missing out, they're not learning and they don't have faith in themselves.

One of my clients was talking to me about being at a conference. During the breaks between lectures, in one of those loud networking sessions, my client found himself talking to some true experts in their field. These people exuded confidence and intelligence and went into huge detail and depth about the subject of the conference. My client was a bit awe-struck, and sometimes he lost the thread of the conversation, or didn't know what to say because he feared it might give away the fact that he was totally out of his depth. As the conversation went on, he got quieter and quieter. He felt flustered, unable to speak, couldn't think of the right words. He came away feeling pretty shit about himself.

I suggested another way to handle this. The tough approach is to pretend to understand but be squirming inside. So instead I said, try smiling and saying "wow, I feel totally out of my depth here and you really seem to know your stuff, could you explain this to me?" In other words, drop the pretence that you are tough, and instead embrace strength through vulnerability. Speak the truth, and see how it changes the situation. Now some people might take advantage there, they might scoff at you. But most won't. Most people will warm to you, because of your honesty and humanity, and they'll be glad and even grateful to share their passion with you.

This kind of strength is adaptable. It's realistic. It fosters connections. It's determined to remain true to yourself and your path, but curious about what's possible. It plays with possibilities. It can't be undermined because it's rooted in your trust that you are ok, no matter what happens.

That is the kind of strength that I want to help you develop through this series.

Setting yourself up to succeed

Things that are worthwhile tend to take time and sustained effort to achieve. Building a successful career, developing trust and companionship with a partner, becoming a good parent, clearing debts, discovering your spiritual expression. Whatever it is, if it's worthwhile then it'll be hard sometimes and keeping moving in the right direction will, at times, be difficult or confusing.

Good choices build on good choices, moments build on moments, effort builds on effort until eventually you reach your goal. Like climbing a ladder, each rung is a minor achievement in itself, and each rung brings you a little bit closer to the top.

One thing that tends to hold us back from success, or convinces us to aim for smaller goals than we're actually capable of, is a lack of consistency in our lives. Life is a complicated and messy business that sometimes knocks us off-course. It is really hard to get moving, but it's even harder to stay motivated, focused and committed as life throws us wildcards and curve balls. We might lose momentum or become distracted, and this makes it that much harder to set ourselves back on the path to achieve our goals. Anyone who's tried to do something difficult over a long period of time has experienced this.

The way you feel every day will change, as will the things you think about. If you remember where you were ten years ago and what you were doing, were the same things important to you then as they are now? Your thoughts and emotions will adapt and change over time. For some people, they change multiple times in a day. So many things influence us: the opinions and attitudes of the people we spend time with; our lifestyle and the shape of our day; the stresses and obligations that we live with; the way we eat and exercise; the beliefs and customs of our culture. Things can happen in your day that that leave you feeling excited and happy, or which leave you exhausted, miserable or feeling negative.

Change is the only sure and constant companion we can expect in our lives. As the saying goes, *this too shall pass*, no matter what 'this' is. A good feeling or a bad one. A friendship or relationship. Our health. Our very lives. Everything that has a beginning has an end.

Throughout our lives we develop experience and skills. For example, if you start a new job you might feel clumsy, confused or overwhelmed by all the new things you're expected to do. But within a short time you'll learn and develop competence, efficiency and skill. Very broadly, our society pays people better, and provides more benefits, for people with more developed skills, in more desirable areas. One of the most common things that holds people in jobs they don't enjoy is how comfortable they've become with their expertise in very specific tasks. If I feel really good at what I do, even if it's not what I really want to be doing with my time, it's tempting to stay and enjoy my hard-won expertise.

We tend to apply the same logic to other things. It's the comfort zone, 'just the way things are' story again. We get to know a partner really well, so that we anticipate their words and moods. We synchronise our lives with theirs. Long after the relationship has ceased to be fulfilling and nourishing, we don't want to make any changes because it's familiar and comfortable. We do the same with friends, with how we treat ourselves, or with our daily routines.

If you do the same things every day, or have very set routines that you know well, doing each task effortlessly, from making breakfast, to getting ready, to your commute, to doing the tasks of your job well, all the way through to your bedtime routine…you will look and feel very competent indeed. You're the master of your world. You do things quickly and efficiently, even if they're complicated and difficult tasks. You make thousands of individual decisions every day and, in general, you handle them very well. They're so familiar that you can make decisions quickly and without a second thought.

Our culture encourages us towards efficiency and routine. There is so much to do, and if you want time to relax at the end of the day then you have to be pretty organised in completing the tasks of the day. Your boss will praise or promote you if you demonstrate efficiency and smooth competence at work. If you want to meet with your friends at the weekend then you're going to need to balance your diary. Our lives tend to be structured, organised, measured and calendarized. We tend to know what we need to do, and how to do it, and how to do it quickly, efficiently and properly.

This is a significant problem for those of us who want to change something important in our lives.

More important than what we do, is how we do it and why

Søren Kierkegaard was a philosopher in Denmark in the 19th Century. He said that most people live like a drunken peasant on a cart, half asleep, letting the donkey wander where it will. Unless we have done some personal development work and made some serious commitments, we tend to meander from place to place, buffeted by life, unaware of where we're going and unconscious of our power to direct our lives. Even those of us who try to make resolutions and positive decisions can easily find ourselves knocked off centre again.

Kierkegaard encouraged his readers to dedicate their lives to something, to become focused on an overall goal or mission. He said that the whole of life can be made *intentional* rather than accidental.

Plato said that an unreflected life is not worth living.

As you'll see when we begin going through the Rules in Book 2, I'm going to promote a particular mindset and attitude. It includes these ideas:

- Growth into true adulthood – getting very clear on the distinction between child and adult life and the determination to manifest a fully adult self.

- Personal power – choosing to believe that our choices dictate the shape our life takes. Having adopted this belief, we find that each choice, in each moment of our lives, contains the power and potential to steer our lives towards the future we want.

- Personal responsibility – all of our choices have consequences and we cannot truly claim our personal power without also owning the results of the things we choose.

- Identifying and letting go of unhelpful beliefs, habits and life strategies – not waiting for somebody or something else to save us or empower us, but taking the initiative to empower ourselves.

The two key attitudes in this journey of *Arete* are Determination and Curiosity,

Determination

I coach people for a living, and I've been doing it a long time. The nature of a coaching session varies massively, and this variety is what keeps the work so incredibly interesting. I will have a client walk into the room who's energised and driven and in a great mood, and quickly we're both on our feet at the whiteboard, scribbling out an amazing plan, exploring ways to solve problems, talking about possibilities. That client walks out and the next walks in. The whole mood is different. This person is actively suffering, and feeling weak and bruised. The session is quiet. We're looking to make sense of an experience. Tears flow in great numbers and they're absolutely ok and welcome. Together, we figure things out and put the events of *now* into context. They walk away feeling a bit more whole than they did. Another client arrives. This one is beginning to realise why their last two marriages have ended in misery, and it was something about them all along, and they're shaken by this reality. We face this truth together. We explore its origins and its nature and what to do instead and how to reach that new approach without falling back into old habits.

Every person brings something different, and each person changes and grows and meets new challenges, so the conversations shift radically. We never run out of things to say, although silence is common. Some people are good at staying on track, some aren't. Some people learn new skills. Some people realise things about themselves that they become determined to change.

It's *hard work*. I don't think anybody comes to see me without a bit of trepidation. We will talk about hardship and heartbreak and tragedy and abandonment and rage and fear. We will directly confront things that have been allowed to fester. I am there to support, to reflect and to challenge. It's intense. I see people at the edge of their comfort zones, or deep into the unknown, and as they learn to trust me, I often see them in a vulnerable, naked way that few other people will ever see.

And so I have a pretty good idea about what works and what doesn't, to keep someone moving in the direction they want to go. I know all the things we tell ourselves, and I know which ones are true and which ones are avoidance.

Determination is one of the two virtues that you need to adopt.

The determination I mean is this: imagine you're walking along a road. As far as you know, this road takes you in the right direction, it heads in the direction you want to be heading. The only way to get there is to move forwards, to keep moving, to put one foot in front of the other, for as long as it takes.

As you set out, you have no idea what waits around the next corner. And you can be pretty sure that things will go wrong along the way. You're going to get tired. You might get distracted. Other people are going to tempt you to change direction, or otherwise complicate things. You might make mistakes or fail at things along the way. You might need to pause and make sure that this is the correct road to reach your destination.

So determination is simply the commitment to keep moving, as all this chaos happens around you. Each day, in each moment, you renew your certainty that you're going to keep moving, keep trying, keep growing.

Complete failure isn't even possible. You're going to try things, and they might work out or they might not. You're going to make mistakes and learn from them. Some of those mistakes are going to hurt, but you're going to weather the hurt, pause for as long as you need to, and then keep moving. Always moving. Always in the direction that's right for you.

Embrace the inevitability of success. We get to know ourselves, understanding our personal foibles, vulnerabilities, trigger points and emotional responses, and we progressively incorporate this information into our planning. But we do all of this in the sure knowledge that we will reach our end goal. There is simply no other possibility. Any failure is temporary, because we'll deal with the fallout, we'll adapt and tomorrow, we'll try again. We never stop moving. Whether it's a single step in a day or a flat-out run, we keep moving.

Even if you know that you won't show up at your best on a given day, even if you're going to do an imperfect job, even though you're bound to make mistakes, you adopt that simple resolution to keep moving. There is no other possibility.

We never settle, we never say "yes ok, this is good enough. It's not what I wanted but it'll do, I'm too tired to keep trying". Never. Pause if you need to. Rest and care for yourself. But never surrender the journey. The steely determination I'm talking about here doesn't allow it.

On days when you feel good, energised, inspired or happy, be determined to apply yourself fully to the challenges of your life. Let your energy flow into your actions and let your choices be positive ones that build towards the life you want. Use this time to plan, to vision the life you want to build, to dream and to get excited about possibilities that might exist for you.

On days when you have less energy, or when you feel overwhelmed, unsteady or filled with doubt, be determined to do what you can. Even if they are very small, take positive steps and make positive choices. The size of the step is not the most important thing. What's important is that you begin to manifest in your life a potent and unrelenting determination to reach your goals. Momentum is important, so keep it pointed in a direction that's positive for you.

It is not a matter of 'if'. It is simply a matter of 'when'.

Or in the words of Master Yoda from Star Wars: "Do, or do not. There is no try."

I try to impart this perspective, this virtue, to all of my coaching clients. Those who are full of energy: be determined to devote every shred of that energy to your journey. Those who are hurting, focus on healing, understanding and resting...in the knowledge that this too is part of the journey. Those who are learning great and important things about themselves, or the world, or their relationship, or about business...fantastic, incorporate that learning into your journey. Keep moving.

Curiosity

And yet, determination alone will bring us a stale life. Pushing forwards, forever? Driven and committed to the inevitability of success? That's not living. That's merely momentum. There must be something to balance up this compulsion, this ferocity, this hardness. There must be play, lightness, gentleness, the appreciation of the moment, wonder, gratitude. While moving forwards is essential, ignoring the beauty of the journey itself is a tragedy. Life is short, and people at the end of their lives consistently report that they wish they'd paid more attention, enjoyed themselves more.

Determination is the fire and the metal that drives us on. But what of the moment?

So, I also encourage this second virtue: curiosity.

Happiness and lightness of spirit are powerful life skills. To be gently curious about anything and everything lends us that lightness. Genuine curiosity says: I want to know more. I want to investigate and play with this thing, and I'm not really attached to the outcome. I just want to understand, to know, the be delighted by knowledge and experience.

It's easy to treat life as a boring obligation, a series of to-do lists, to dismiss the extraordinary happening around us all the time. As an antidote to this, the French philosopher Paul Ricoeur suggested something called the *Second Naivety*.

In our youth, we are genuinely naïve. We don't know how the world works, so we're curious about everything. Children explore, they turn rocks over to see what's underneath, they make fantasy worlds and tell stories with their toys. They wonder about things.

As we get older, we gain knowledge and we believe we know how the world works. So many people get very attached to their knowledge and become rigid, cynical, and lose their sense of wonder or appreciation for simple things. Life for these people becomes a dry and lifeless place. Again, this is assisted by a dry and unimaginative culture. Most people aren't religious any more, so they don't learn awe and wonder that way. People who are emotionally unfulfilled will tend to become cynical or bitter or disengaged. The world today makes it very easy to live a boring, stale life, and to forget about play and curiosity.

This isn't inevitable, and it isn't the end of the line. While most people do stop here, there is another way. We can choose to maintain the knowledge that we've gained, but to re-learn the curiosity and wonder that we had as children. In this state we find ourselves much more emotionally present and more appreciative of simple things. We're also much more likely to learn. We relinquish our attachment to our hard-won expertise and the single perspective that we've developed, and we welcome information and learning from every possible source.

So, we aim to foster this curiosity every day. When you speak to somebody, get curious about their life and their point of view. So long as this person isn't actively toxic, leave yourself behind for a moment and get into their world-view. What matters to them? What are their priorities? What can you learn from them?

Explore alternative routes to work. Sign up to random classes. Watch some live music. Get interested about what's going on in your town, in your community, in the local park. Pause to watch how trees move in the wind, or the shape of clouds, or the hard work of ants. Notice your feelings, or the sensations of your body, or the workings of your mind. Learn how things are done, and why. Get interested in history, or politics, or art, or ikebana flower arranging. There is so much happening around us all the time, there is never a reason to be bored.

Try to see things as if for the first time. That old building you see every day. The face of your partner. Treasured old possessions.

It's less about what you learn, and more about training your mind to be inquisitive. A curious mind is adaptable. A curious mind becomes full of interesting things. A curious mind solves problems in creative ways. A curious person is often fun to be around.

We become more flexible, adaptable people by embracing a curiosity about life, and we end up more interesting, more knowledgeable, stronger and ultimately more successful as a result. But greater than that is the deepening of experience that we gain. The world feels more alive, we notice more, we stop letting life rush past.

Curiosity is a great companion on this journey, and I really encourage you to foster it.

Self-mastery begins with self-knowledge

We're complex creatures. I want to talk a little bit about the makeup of the human person, because it's going to be important that we've got a shared understanding as we go deeper into this journey together. There is so much that we're not taught: our culture is not designed to help us understand ourselves.

As I've said already, we're basically just mammals with big brains. But the interplay between the three main areas of the brain and the body, plus layers of instinct, intuition and indoctrination, create a very complex model indeed. We are physical, and emotional, and mental, and spiritual.

How normal became so toxic

Our culture, and our modern lifestyles, and the unique fears and pressures of this time in history, put specific pressures on us. Animals that were already unusual (thanks to our big brains) now also have to deal with persistent stress. We stress about challenges and problems at work. We stress about conflicts in our relationships. We stress about juggling all the complex moving pieces in our lives. We stress about having fun!

Stress is a natural response to threat and danger. It's a very predictable pattern of hormones and reactions in our bodily tissues, which then translate into thoughts and responses and feelings. Stress is a leading cause of illness. It was never meant to be a long-term experience, it's designed to be a short term response to danger, not a way of life. Over time it causes a whole host of different medical problems, and we know this. We can feel our blood pressure climbing, we can track our sleepless nights, we know what anxiety feels like. So, collectively, we have adapted.

One of the way we cope in this stress-filled culture is to encourage those around us to behave themselves, in all sorts of subtle ways. Our children laugh at kids who are different, or bully those who stand out. So we learn not to stand out. At work, we generally don't want people showing emotion or acting up, so there are workplace cultures that ensure everyone behaves in a certain way. People can have decades-long relationships and yet never really meet, because they are both pretending to be someone that is appealing to the other person, and they encourage each other to keep wearing their masks. We often seek peace in our lives by wearing our masks and by encouraging other people to do the same. Be simple, be predictable, be quiet.

As soon as you understand the masks you wear in order to keep yourself and others in safe, predictable boxes, you have the option to remove your masks and begin getting to know this vastly complex, fascinating person underneath. At first, this tends to be scary and unpredictable and wild. You will stand out. You will rock boats. You will ask uncomfortable questions. You might need to face a lot of difficult emotions without a mask to soften your experience. Eventually you will learn much more effective ways to navigate life, including better ways to handle stress, but it does cause a lot of disruption on the way to that level of self-mastery.

What most people do, instead of embarking on this remarkable journey, is make a deal with themselves and with everyone else in their lives. It's better, they say to each other, to have a shared status quo, a world of people wearing masks and following pre-defining patterns of words, choices and behaviour. Let's not make this life more difficult than it has to be. Let's not introduce more stress here. Let's keep things safe.

The reality of a human being is complex and passionate and does not fit into the narrow boxes of our society. To begin removing our masks is disruptive, it is difficult and so most people choose instead to live safer lives behind their masks.

So we walk around, trapped in simplified, limited versions of ourselves. We did this to ourselves, and we continue to do it to ourselves every day. We create for ourselves a restricted, truncated, stunted, constrained version of who we could be. Our potential, creativity, emotional expression, the satisfaction of our fundamental needs and our uniqueness are all sacrificed.

We do this from a deep need to be loved and accepted. To be human is to have intrinsic human needs. They are part of our DNA, and some of our needs include:

- The need to be loved

- The need to feel safe

- The need for positive feedback from other people

So in a culture where it's normal to wear masks, the most obvious route to getting our intrinsic needs satisfied is to wear a mask, to pretend to be someone you're not. To wear a mask is normal, and if I am normal then perhaps I will be accepted and loved.

Unfortunately, it's a strategy that's doomed to fail. Living behind a mask isn't really living. Our real needs will never get satisfied. We can never truly be happy like this.

Equipping yourself for the journey

Throughout our lives we find moments of clarity where we're shown the bizarre nature of the masks we wear. Sometimes these moments are brief: an overheard conversation, a moment of seeing people living another way. Sometimes they come about through times of trauma or moments of bliss or peak experiences. But, tragically, it's most often found at the very end of life. The profound trauma and dread as we approach death is, in fact, the unveiling of a lifelong desire: the need to exist, to be our true selves, to truly exist in a moment, a place, amongst a people who love and accept us for who we really are.

We are all naturally drawn to undertake a journey of personal awakening. We know, deep down, that pretending to be a simpler version of ourselves will never really satisfy us. It's safe, it's known, and the comfort zone is always tempting. But what we really *need is to be* loved and accepted *for who we really are*, and this will never be possible as long as we wear conscious and unconscious masks. Removing those masks requires skills. So our need for love, belonging and deeper fulfilment eventually become our need to undertake the journey to meet our true selves.

Many pre-modern cultures seem to contain a prebuilt mechanism to do this. There were vision quests, rites of initiation, core mythologies and stories that at once entertained, but also provided a framework for someone to work out who they really are. Rituals and beliefs and habits existed that equipped each person with the tools they would need on their journey to figure out who they are.

In our culture, of course, none of this exists. The reasons for that are complex. We have rejected a lot of the older lessons of traditional religions, often for good reasons. Our development of science and psychology has left us sceptical of a lot of quick or simple answers. And the overwhelming, overbearing presence of capitalist marketing turns our lives into marketplaces, and every solution to our unhappiness into a product, screaming for our attention, promising to be *the thing* that will make us feel better.

So if we want to do this work, to undertake this journey of getting to know our true solves, we have to make time for it separate from our work and daily life. The fact that we have to do this shows just how profoundly our culture fails to meet our most fundamental needs. I'll be talking a lot about the toxic stories buried within our culture in this book.

The first steps on each person's journey tend to be external. The comfort zone is powerful. We cling to things that feel safe. It tends to take a wake up call, or the inspiration from another human being, or a tragedy, or some kind of disruption which forces us to finally admit that the journey is waiting for us, that it matters, and that we must begin.

Once this has happened, it's handy to begin assembling a toolkit. Learn the building blocks of you. Understand the nature and shape of the self. Knowing what you are is a great foundation to begin your journey. So that's the point of the next chapter. I'm going to break off pieces of the human person, name them, and give you a bunch of information about each. I'm also going to name core skills you're going to need.

Your toolkit

This whole book is designed to equip you with the essential knowledge to undertake a successful journey of personal development. Every day, I meet with people who are seeking change, and a big part of my job is to spot the gaps in their knowledge. What did their father never say to them? What was missing in their education? What painful beliefs have they carried through lives which can be dispelled with a simple piece of information, or a simple bit of theory? And, what do I wish I'd known when I was walking my own journey?

In this chapter I'll be exploring a lot of common words or ideas from psychology and coaching. I'm sure you'll have heard most of these ideas, but it's important to have a clear understanding of what they really mean, and how they fit in to your journey. My job is all about keeping things practical, so I'll also be offering advice about how to handle things, or ways you can explore further.

Self-image

Self-image is a thing that you already have. For many of us, it's a deeply precious thing that we work hard to maintain and protect.

Self-image is the person you think you are. It is the image you have of yourself in your mind, in your feelings and in your body. It is the person you believe that you are, that you feel you are.

You say to yourself: I know who I am because recognise these things about myself. It's how I know who I am.

I do these things, I believe these things, I talk like this, I can do these things, these are my limitations.

Self-image is your idea of who and what you are.

It may be completely wrong.

The building-blocks of self-image

This idea of self-image is built from a lot of things.

For example, your memories and experiences form part of your idea of who you are. You draw on all the moments of joy, pain, triumph, failure, disappointment, satisfaction, gladness and desolation that you've lived. Your memories are part of how you define who you are. You remember how you handled situations, how you reacted, what happened to you, and this informs who you believe yourself to be.

Self-image also comes from how you currently relate to people around you. Are you the kind of person who, when arriving in a room full of people, will feel excited to go around shaking hands, exchanging names, making new connections? Or does this situation make you tremble or feel uncomfortable? Do you put huge effort into just a few, precious relationships or do you get happiness and satisfaction from knowing a wide range of people who you prefer to keep at a bit of a distance? Perhaps a bit of both? When intimate with someone, do you want to throw yourself in deep, becoming an open book, sharing all that you are, or do you prefer to keep a part of yourself withheld and just for yourself? These kinds of instincts in relationships are part of the way you identify yourself.

The person you imagine yourself to be is also defined by the work you do, how you do it, and how you are regarded in the eyes of society at large. You define yourself this way. Do you earn well, in a job that brings you respect and approval? Do you work hard, gaining satisfaction from the quality of your work? Is work a secondary thing for you, just a thing that has to be done in order to pay the bills? Do you avoid work entirely? Are you prevented from working by something? Do you do something else with your time, which you struggle to label as 'work'? Do you see yourself as a success or a failure? What would other people say?

Your self-image is also defined by all of the areas where you believe you're skilled or unskilled. From baking to driving, from making coffee to making conversation, from dancing to painting, from IT to gardening, from meticulous planning to the ability to truly and deeply let go and relax. There are so many things that you might believe you're good at, and so many that you probably believe you do badly. These beliefs all contribute to our image of ourselves.

You receive aspects of your self-image from your culture. We think of ourselves as coming from a country, with certain laws, traditions, customs and language. We will tend towards a certain view of the world, of history, of believing people from other countries, languages and traditions are better or worse than we are. People from the same culture tend to dress similarly, tend to display wealth and prosperity in certain ways and tend to have similar ideas about education, how politics should work, how human beings should relate to the natural world. We might be very proud of our country or feel ashamed of the way it behaves. We might work hard to fit in with rules and expectations or we might try to break them. Whatever your relationship with the culture around you, it will feed into how you think and feel about who you are.

Self-image is physically embodied as well. The way you hold yourself when you walk and stand, your body language during conversations, the way you breathe, where and how you hold tension in your body. Do you see yourself as graceful and aware of your body, or is your body just a clumsy thing that carries your consciousness around?

Do you tend to breathe in short, shallow gasps, or do you breathe fully into the whole of your lungs with slow and purposeful breaths?

These are just some examples of things that contribute to your sense of who you are.

The crucial thing to understand about self-image is that it's not who you are. It's who you *believe* you are.

You will have a mental picture of yourself as someone who does some things, doesn't do other things, speaks in a certain way, thinks in a certain way, breathes in a certain way. This is a deeper level of the 'just the way things are' story from chapter two.

A vital step in coming home to the person you were meant to be, the person you truly are, is to begin discovering your own authentic self-image. Abandoning labels and images that you've been given and searching for your own idea of who you are. This will allow you to begin unlocking your awareness of your genuine self.

This curiosity and willingness will open up the opportunity for you to change your self-image, and thus redefine the limits of what you can achieve.

Compassionate Non-judgement

In this journey towards your personal *Arete*, we're going to meet uncomfortable or challenging things. There are always parts of us that we'd rather not look at, things that we've done that we feel ashamed of, things that we find unacceptable but which exist deep within us. Everybody has this. Over the course of this book we'll examine why, but I just want to offer you some reassurance that if this happens to you, it's not a bad sign. It's entirely normal.

Equally, there are things we are very fond of in ourselves. Maybe you're particularly gifted at something, or perhaps you're very proud of a certain thing that you do. It can be very tempting to look at these things for a long time and just bask in the feeling of pride. That's not a bad thing, but it can stop us from wanting to dig deeper into the whys and the underpinning truths. I'm going to be inviting you to dig deep during our journey together. We're looking for a radical honesty with ourselves.

Other things inside us might be boring, frustrating, frightening, painful or feel dangerous or reckless.

The skill that we all need to develop in order to safely do this inner work, is the skill of compassionate non-judgement. This skill also tends to dramatically improve our relationships with others. I'll be offering you ideas and resources to develop your own sense of compassionate non-judgement.

We are explorers in an inner landscape, and as explorers we don't judge what we find. We simply observe and understand. The best attitude to adopt in this work is one of compassion. If I learn that a part of me is petty, or selfish, or wants to hurt other people, then I regard that part of myself with compassion and just seek to understand it. I don't label it as good or bad, because I know that any labels are going to limit my ability to understand. Things within ourselves are neither positive or negative: it's their effects and the actions that they lead us to perform that we must learn to control, and our self-control will grow with our knowledge. What lies beneath simply is.

Similarly, if I notice parts of myself that are beautiful, courageous, graceful or noble, then I regard them with exactly the same kind of non-judgemental compassion. I cultivate a deep curiosity about the whole of myself, from the very 'best' parts to the very 'worst' parts. This complex and multifaceted being is who I am, and judging or suppressing parts of who I am does not stop them being true. It just limits my ability to learn.

Later in this book we'll look at what we're going to *do* with all this stuff that we find. For now, we are simply exploring and trying to understand. I believe, having spent hundreds of hours of my life with people exploring this landscape, that our deepest and most fundamental motivations are basically good, and that the negative and harmful things that we find within ourselves are all attempts to meet forgotten or neglected needs, where the attempts have gone wrong somehow. So I invite you to trust that your inner landscape rests on healthy foundations, and that underneath things that might be uncomfortable or difficult, even frightening, we will find beautiful and good roots.

I want to add that nothing in this book should be taken as judgement upon you. I offer you the same kind of compassionate non-judgement that I encourage you to offer yourself. I will be showing you things that might be challenging or emotionally triggering, but these too are delivered without judgement.

The tree of self

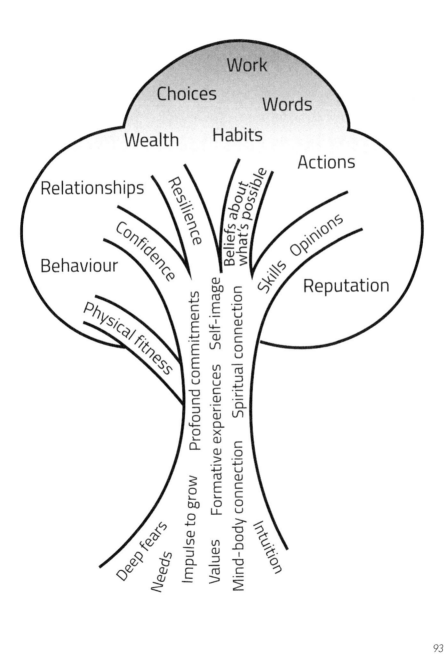

We exist on many levels. When I choose to do something, or when I do something without noticing, there will have been a reason for it. We do nothing without a reason, even if that reason is as simple as: I scratched because I had an itch. Many clients who come to see me begin by telling me about things that they've done, or which have happened to them, and when I ask why these things happened they tell me 'they just did' or 'no reason'. I always say that we do everything for a reason. It's an important assumption to make. If we believe we do things without any reason, there's nothing to examine, understand, learn or overcome. If we believe that there's a reason behind everything we do, it becomes our job to understand all of our motivations, and the knowledge we gain is hugely empowering.

Some of the things that motivate and drive us don't even exist any more: something was right for us once, and we keep responding in the same way. For example, we might spend years with a partner who makes unkind comments about our appearance. You adapt, either trying to look nice for them or giving up on looking nice altogether. Later, you break up but you continue to behave in the same way. Each morning you get ready, or keep asking for the same haircut, but the original motivator has gone. You've settled into a pattern.

However, each time we recycle choices which have ceased to be relevant for us, we have the option to choose to do something else instead. Everything is choice: some part of us chose to say that word, or perform that action, or think that thought, or make that choice.

Some motivations sit closer to the surface than others. Some impulses are obvious and we tend to be pretty aware of them. When we take the time to examine these motivations, we tend to find that they sit upon other, deeper and more fundamental ones. Often, these sit upon deeper still and more profound reasons.

As an example, let's go back to the choice to make an effort to look nice. One day, I choose to wear nice clothes, take care of my personal grooming, get a nice haircut. It's something we all do sometimes – some of us do it more often than others. But it takes effort: it's an active choice.

The obvious surface motivations are that it feels good, and I like the responses I get from others. People might comment on the way I look. I catch a glimpse of myself in the mirror and I like what I see. Perhaps somebody is attracted to the way I look and a new connection is formed that brings all kinds of possibilities with it. By taking this action, I get a range of positive, warming sensations which all came about because I made a certain choice. I hoped these things would happen, which is why I made the choice I did.

But is that it? Does that tell us everything about the reason I choose to make an effort with my appearance?

This is where the tree metaphor comes in. At first we notice the branches of the tree. In this example our branches are called positive self-regard, words of affirmation from others, and possibilities for intimacy and connection. Those are the reasons for the choices I've made.

The branches of a tree are supported by its limbs, boughs and trunk, and the same goes for our motivations. Under every surface impulse are deeper reasons. The deeper we understand our reasons for doing things, the more awareness we have of ourselves and the more power we have to change. If we've been stuck in patterns of behaviour for our whole lives then it will take some courageous, deep searching to uncover why, and then choose to do something different.

We've identified the surface motivations in our example of choosing to make an effort with appearance, so what do they rest upon? What deeper reasons hold the branches of positive self-regard, words of affirmation and intimacy?

It may be that I am masking my insecurities. I may carry a sense of shame or a dislike of myself, and it's important for me to make an effort to mask this. Perhaps I believe that my ability to succeed in the ways that are important for me depends on the way I look. Maybe my parents drilled into me the importance of appearance based on their own experiences or insecurities, and I've just carried their priorities through my life. Maybe I was shamed or attacked once for not looking right, so I dress carefully to avoid more conflict or shame. What if there's somebody in particular that I want to impress? Or perhaps I am trying to shore up a certain kind of prestige or model of success: people who succeed dress like this, don't they?

When I'm stressed and struggling, looking nice might be the only way I have to reassure myself that I'm doing well. It could be that I don't even notice the clothes I wear, and I'm confused or annoyed that people respond to me differently depending on how I look. It could even be that I don't get to choose what I wear: perhaps work or my situation in life dictates the way I dress, and that leaves me feeling in a certain way.

These are just some possibilities that exist for this one choice.

Judgement and self-deceit

Often, self-image will be deeply cherished. It can feel very important to know who we are, to know what we're good and bad at, to know how we relate to people and how people see us. Even if we believe that we're incompetent, or bad, or a failure, or some other negative thing, it's still basically comfortable. We know where we stand.

We're heavily invested in these ideas of ourselves and our place in the world. It gives us security and reassurance. Often, we will have invested so much time, energy and intention in fighting to protect this version of ourselves. We don't want all that energy to have been a waste!

It's understandable that we might work hard to protect our sense of self-image. Many people go to great lengths to protect themselves from being challenged in their beliefs about themselves. Perhaps they immediately reject somebody's ideas if they don't fit how they see themselves. Perhaps they only spend time with a certain kind of person, or go to places that feel familiar. Perhaps they avoid using their bodies in new ways, and would reject an invitation to a gym, a dance class, a meditation retreat or a martial arts hall. Perhaps they judge people who dress differently. Perhaps they only spend time with people of a similar age group or political persuasion.

We get settled into patterns of behaviour very easily. It's the 'just the way things are' story again. We will often fight fiercely to protect our ideas about ourselves. Here are some of the things we say to fend off suggestions that we might loosen our grip on a fixed idea of who we are:

'I'm just not like that!'

'I don't do things like that!'

'I'm too shy for that.'

'I'm too good for that.'

'What a stupid thing for somebody to do.'

'Oh I could never do that!'

'I just don't have the time.'

'Well that's fine for some people but it's not right for me!'

Judgement is the ultimate defence against a challenge to self-image. We can become so attached to our ideas about who we are that we feel we need to attack those who are different, to prove to ourselves and others that we aren't like them. This need to judge people, to categorise them in broad and sweeping ways that erase individuality and turn complex and interesting people into just a member of a group, is a demonstration of basic insecurity. The weaker and less explored your self-image, the more likely you are to be judgemental. Something challenges an aspect of our self-image, and we fear its loss, so we remove the challenge by turning the person saying it into something non-human, something easily dismissed. We might group them as 'idiots', 'fools', 'posh people', 'rich, privileged people', 'hippies' or 'drop-outs'. We might judge them as much less intelligent than we are. We might judge them as failures, or people who have made stupid mistakes in their lives. They might be the wrong religion, the wrong class, the wrong colour, the wrong political affiliation or the wrong sexuality. Whatever we decide they are, we stop them being a challenge to the nice, reassuring things we believe about ourselves by removing their humanity and assigning them a label instead.

We might also go to great lengths to deceive ourselves, to build up a self-image that has very little to do with reality. Are you really as smart, skilled and competent as you think you are? Or perhaps you think the opposite: are you really as stupid, as unskilled and as incompetent as you think you are?

One of the core messages here is that self-image can change. You do not have to be who you have always been. But more than that: holding tightly to a fixed idea of who you are will stifle your growth and will encourage you to judge others and miss out on great opportunities.

I invite you to treat the person you think you are as an idea. Hold it lightly. Investigate it. Allow yourself to be surprised. Be willing to confront the parts of yourself that have stagnated or held you back. For some people in our culture, there's an illusion that it's a virtue to be stubborn, unyielding and unwilling to change. In my experience, the opposite is true. A person who is strong and successful, who is real and present and dependable, is somebody who is able to shift and change over time. They have become conscious and aware of who they truly are through a programme of challenging inner and outer growth. But they are always willing to learn more, to discover that they were wrong about themselves, and to make changes in the light of new information.

This, as we'll discuss, is true strength.

The three paths on the one journey

As I've mentioned, there are three paths that you will need to walk on your journey: Being (your inner development), Doing (the effects you have in the world) and Relating (how you relate to other living beings).

Uncovering your current self-image (the person you think you are) will involve exploring all three paths. In this chapter I'll be looking at the inner aspects of your self but we'll come back to self-image throughout this series of books, and we'll look at how Doing and Relating contribute to who we think we are. For now, here are some simple ideas of things from the Doing and Relating paths that go into self-image:

The outer path:

- The work you do
- Your hobbies and how much energy you devote to them
- How you relax, how often you rest
- Your exercise routine
- The things you own, collect, accrue and how you use them.
- Your car
- Your home
- Your daily routine, like the route you take to work
- Your holidays

The path of relating:

- Your intimate partner
- The rituals of love that exist in your relationship(s)
- The depth of your trust and vulnerability with others
- The way you are intimate
- The way you are romantic
- How you interpret and expect love
- The friends you have, how often you connect with them and what these relationships are like
- The levels of contact and sharing that exist throughout your life

Inner aspects of self

The rest of this chapter will set out a common language for us to speak about aspects and areas of ourselves. Each of these areas offer you new opportunities for discovery, awakening and personal growth. Some people find one aspect so compelling, or so in need of their attentions, that they'll dedicate their entire lives to its study. But more often, we each need to delve a little into each aspect of ourselves. I have never met anyone who did not need to explore each aspect below, at least a little. There are certain signs that you are called to delve into a particular aspect of your self. As you read, observe your own responses. Practise the compassionate non-judgment that we've spoken about. Watch out for feelings of annoyance, boredom, anger, discomfort, inadequacy, yearning, fascination or excitement. Any of these might be a sign that you are called to explore this aspect of yourself more fully.

Language is very important. Since humans began using it to structure the way we think, our thoughts and intentions have been bound up with the meaning of the words we use. A subtle difference in the way that we speak about ourselves can transform the way that we feel and the way we appear to others. Confusion, conflict and poisoned relationships arise from the wrong words. So at the beginning of this journey together, I will lay out some language that we can be sure we both understand.

Mind

Depending on where you grew up, you'll understand your mind in completely different ways. Eastern religions, particularly Buddhism, have a very different understanding of the mind from the one we have in Western countries. If you'd grown up in certain parts of India, Nepal, Tibet or Thailand, your 'just the way things are' would include a radically different belief about the nature of mind. Buddhism can reasonably be called a two-and-a-half-thousand-year-old scientific enquiry into the nature of the mind. Unfortunately, in the West we tend to enshrine the mind as a thing of great value without really trying to understand it. We confuse the mind with the brain, and we confuse the mind with consciousness. *Thinking about* something is often confused with *being* something.

An old teacher of mine, a Buddhist who had dedicated his life to travel and to meditation, studying with gurus in India and Tibet, would refer to the mind as a 'repeating engine'. The mind is something that repeats things it's already learned. In the minds of many people there is a constant babble and chatter which is made up of old conversations, old ideas, old memories or parts of songs. This chatter is so normal to us that we barely notice it most of the time. In busy lives spent in busy towns and cities, there is almost always noise going on and we mirror this with our internal noise.

In my experience, and in the experience of everyone I've met who has explored their own relationship to their mind, the mind is the part of us that thinks things through, that orders and aligns the world to make sense to us, that makes plans and lists, that imagines future scenarios, that uses logic, that solves problems. It is a complex, organic calculator that uses information we've learned and retained in order to solve the problems that we meet. The mind is not the brain. Modern science has shown that the brain is probably the organ that gives rise to most aspects of the mind, but the mind is a thing we experience. I feel my mind, I do not feel my brain. That said, there are a lot of features of the brain that carry over into the nature of mind. For example, the brain tends to form pathways, which it strengthens over time if it uses those pathways a lot, like a worn path that becomes a road that becomes a highway as it used more and more. These become the most efficient routes between two places: well-worn and neurologically developed. So it is with the mind. When we become used to thinking in certain ways, we tend towards repeating those thoughts again. The mind likes to repeat things, and only with sustained effort to shift our thinking to a new place will we let go of our old patterns of thought.

As far as personal development and awakening are concerned, the most important things to know about the mind are:

- thinking is addictive, and

- we are not our minds.

A meaningless babble goes on in the mind a lot of the time. Generally, we don't notice it. But if you've ever tried to clear your mind after a busy or stressful day, you'll notice how loud the babble has become. We tend to get attached to these thoughts and pay them a lot of attention, and we tend to take them very seriously. We play along with the memories and join in the conversations. We talk to ourselves. We can become just as emotionally triggered by an old conversation or an imagined situation in the future as we can from a real situation. For anybody who struggles with anxiety, you'll know the dread of something that hasn't even happened yet, and might never happen. But none of this exists, here and now. We only truly exist in a single moment that we call 'now'. That is the most real thing we can experience. Why is it, then, that we can find things in the mind impact us so strongly?

We'll be focusing a lot in this book on the toxic nature of modern culture. One way that it hurts us is by massively over-inflating the value of the mind. Remember that the mind is just a repeating, planning, thinking engine. Very useful for problem solving, but that's all that it does. There is an old phrase: "to a man with a hammer, everything looks like a nail". In a thinking-addicted culture, everything looks like a problem to solve. We have developed jobs, entertainment, an education system and a language that is heavily skewed towards using the mind. Our money and wealth are ideas far more than they are tangible things. This is a major reason why we cause so much harm to the natural world that we depend on for our lives: we are not really here! We are not rooted in the moment, connected with the living world and with one another. We are not feeling, experiencing or being. We are away in our minds, chasing a thought, a memory or an imagined future. We think, we plan, we remember, we fantasise.

Thinking is addictive, and if you were brought up in addiction and if you've never known anything else, it's hard work to shake the habit. Somebody asks you to plan something at work: you need to think. You want to socialise with your friends so you go to see a movie: you're taken out of your body into a fantasy of the mind. Entire relationships can be spent between two people who barely notice each other, but are caught up in their imagination about what's actually happening in the relationship. Old friends meet and repeat the same ideas at each other. We tend to wake up thinking, spend most of the day in the mind, and unwind at the end of the day by doing mind-led things.

This has become so ubiquitous and so normalised that we rarely stop to notice that we are not actually our minds. The mind is a thing that you have. A very useful, very distracting aspect of self which wants to snare your attention. The mind is jealous of your attention and wants to keep as much of it as possible. So the boundaries between consciousness and mind are forgotten or ignored. The 'I', the part of us that exists in the moment and oversees our whole selves, is drowned out by the babble of the mind.

In the 16th Century, René Descartes wrote "I think, therefore I am". He was talking about what we can prove and what we can be sure of. So much of what we believe or experience cannot be *proven* to exist, but one thing must be true: in order for somebody to wonder if the world exists, in order for there to be a consciousness capable of asking any of these questions or observing anything at all, there must be an 'I'. If I am having thoughts, I must exist. Hence: I think, therefore I am.

But it seems to me that there's a problem with this phrase. Descartes' famous phrase only exists if you believe you are your mind. If he'd been able to spend some time with a Tibetan Buddhist of his time, already far more advanced in the science of the mind, he might have written his most famous phrase differently. He might have written 'I observe, therefore I am.'

He might even have written, 'I think, therefore I am not.'

We tend to confuse the 'I', the conscious awareness that allows us to perceive anything at all, with the mind.

At this point, at the boundary between thinking and being, language begins to fail us because language is a construct of the mind. Thankfully, the tools that allow us to directly witness the difference between mind and consciousness are becoming very popular and easily accessible.

Your own exploration

The scientific study of mind, passed down to us through the Buddhist tradition, has given us a process to be able to observe our own minds without attaching to the thoughts and losing our identity once more amid its babble. This tool is called meditation.

There are dozens of kinds of meditation and each tries to achieve something different. Some are reflections on a certain topic, like the Sufi Muraqabah. Some are mystical rituals that try to access things normally hidden from us. Buddhism itself is fragmented into many branches and traditions, from the semi-magical traditions of Tibet to the ascetic traditions of Zen. The problem is that all of these approaches to meditation carry a set of beliefs and values with them.

They carry with them the expectation that you are going to buy-in to a belief structure.

There is value to this, but here we are trying to understand the nature of the mind and begin teasing apart the conscious self from the thinking self. So I tend to recommend a modern tradition called Mindfulness, which one meditation master I learned from called "Buddhist practice without the Buddhism" or "Buddhism Lite". Mindful meditation is becoming very popular. You will probably find a local Mindfulness group or class, you can find Mindful meditations available online and there are free apps that you can download. Some businesses bring in Mindfulness experts or teachers to support their staff.

We'll look at Mindfulness in more detail later in this book, but it's so easily accessed that you can start exploring it as soon as you want. It uses simple techniques like body scanning and listening to the breath to lure your conscious attention away from its fascination with the mind. Given enough time and a sustained, determined practice you'll begin to notice how separate the mind is from the part of you that's doing the observing. This is, for many people, a transformational awakening in itself, and it opens up many possibilities.

In order to discover the nature of 'I', the core self that sits at the heart of the kaleidoscope that is you, you will need to relinquish attachment to the idea that you are your mind. This can only be done through experience, and Mindfulness meditation is the best experience I know to allow you to learn about the nature of mind. It may not happen quickly – the greatest benefits of Mindfulness happen over time. If you haven't already, I invite you to explore the nature of mind by committing to a regular Mindfulness practice.

Emotion

Emotion is separate from mind and it follows different rules. Where mind is a repeating engine and a mechanism that is removed from the here-and-now, emotions exist in the present moment. While philosophers, psychologists and neuroscientists have been writing about how we feel for a long time, they've generally done it from the perspective of a thought-addicted culture. For this reason, several things have warped our personal exploration of our emotional aspect.

The first is a very old prejudice around gender. In our culture, women are believed to be emotional where men are rational. Second, and linked to the first, is the idea that thinking is superior to feeling. These two prejudices work together to create a lot of judgements around gender and emotion: women are irrational; men should be emotionless; emotional people are stupid and useless; emotionless people are intelligent and reliable. If you listen carefully, you'll hear these prejudices behind all sorts of things that people say.

For these reasons, there's actually very little information about what emotions are. There are lots of books about mastering your emotions, suppressing them, conquering them, escaping them, but these books lack the fundamental understand of what emotions are, what they're for, what they do for you and how to harness the strengths and skills they bring you.

I am tired of this gap in our knowledge. It causes so much needless suffering and confusion in people, and it's a big part of why our culture is so incredibly destructive to the natural world that sustains us. Our mind-addicted culture, caught up in thoughts and plans that don't exist here and now, does terrible damage to the planet. Mountains levelled for the minerals they contain. Rivers polluted. Ecosystems ravaged. Entire species exterminated. Islands of plastic floating in the oceans. Rising global temperatures that threaten runaway destruction. Realistic projections are forecasting a very difficult future for our children.

All of this is the work of a culture that thinks rather than exists. Emotions are a way back to sanity, a way to relate better to other people, a way to develop true strength and a vital part of empathy and conscious living.

Emotions arise out of the part of our brain that we share with other mammals, meaning we feel basically the same things they feel. Each emotion is a shortcut to certain vital information about what's happening to use, and each emotion has a function and purpose.

Emotions, then, can be described as messengers from deep and wise parts of ourselves. They are at once fairly simplistic, and bring us a great deal of information. Each emotion exists to serve you in a specific way, to bring your attention to something that's happening, to restore some imbalance in your life.

They are simplistic because they simply do what they do. They are not malleable in the way thoughts are, we cannot mould them into convenient shapes because we don't like the shape they already have. Anger feels like anger, fear will always feel the way fear feels and happiness will continue to feel happy no matter what you do. Situations happen, and when we don't meet those situations from our deepest awareness and with profound wisdom, our emotions respond to help us. Nobody has the awareness to always respond perfectly to every situation, so the emotions within us act like guardians and helpers to bring us back to the moment and attend to it properly.

Emotions are not always convenient or well behaved. If we are living in ways that don't fulfil all our needs, our emotions will remind us about this regularly. If we make choices that are harmful, or which don't honour our true selves, our emotions might be chaotic and confusing, as each feeling tries to respond to some aspect of our bad decisions. If you find your feelings confusing, uncomfortable or baffling, I strongly encourage you to begin learning to listen out for what they're telling you. For many of my coaching clients, learning the messages carried by their emotions was the most radically freeing and exciting thing they'd ever done. It all finally made sense, and guided by the wisdom of their emotions they naturally began living more empowered, happier, calmer lives.

Emotions bring us the skill of empathy. Where mind fails to understand another person, empathy connects us. Where words are clumsy and wrong, empathy communicates without language. Through empathy we come to know another person in a deep and compassionate way without knowing specific facts about them. When I see a person who is suffering, and I allow myself to connect empathetically, I am with them in their suffering. From this place I will relate to them with far more skill and kindness than I would by merely observing their struggle. With a connection of empathy, we allow emotions to flow, to be witnessed, to be grounded, and to be released.

Emotions are supposed to flow into our lives, share their message, be recognised and understood, and then flow on, leaving us calm. The problems that many people experience with their emotions are the result of these steps being interrupted somehow. Perhaps too many emotions are arriving at once and it's overwhelming. Perhaps you don't know how to receive the information that an emotion is giving you. Perhaps you can't or won't take the action that your feelings are encouraging you to take.

Emotions are profoundly wise because they are constantly offering us information that will drop us more deeply into the present moment, and often they're offering us solutions to problems that the mind can't solve. Karla McLaren, an author and teacher, is a world-renowned expert on the subject of emotions. Her book, *The Language of Emotions*, is a practical guide to the origin, nature and function of each major emotion, and of developing skills in emotional awareness and empathy. I have used her ideas with men to help them break out of the emotional straight-jacket that our culture puts on men, and with women to legitimise the role of emotion in living, learning and healing, restoring it from the cultural judgements of silliness, confusion or irrelevance. She is the teacher that I recommend to anyone who want to understand and unleash the power of their emotions.

Further exploration

The work of unlearning old stories about the nature of emotion, and of learning to respect and listen to the messages carried by each emotion, is a massive challenge for most of us, but one that we must each engage with to overcome our personal patterns and to begin making better, more consistent choices in our lives.

I know of no better place to start than Karla McLaren's book *The Language of Emotions*. I also recommend that you begin to observe your language and beliefs around your feelings and the feelings of others. Are you carrying outdated ideas about the value of emotions? Do you judge or mock people for the emotions they feel? Do you judge or persecute yourself when you feel things that are inconvenient?

Body

For a mind-addicted culture, the body is the thing that you see when you look down. From this perspective, there are two functions for the body: to do all the unimportant biological stuff that's necessary so that we can keep thinking, and to carry around the consciousness so we can do all the things that we've thought about. As we've become aware of the obesity epidemic, and of rising levels of certain lifestyle-related diseases, we've realised that we need to put more effort into keeping the body healthy so that it can keep fulfilling its two basic functions. We're also fully aware of good and bad sensations that the body gives the mind to work with. We want more of the good experiences (things like tasty food, nice sensations, sex, the positive feelings when somebody says our body looks nice) and we want less of the bad experiences (physical pain, stiff joints, embarrassment, disease, limited freedom and death). That is about as far as most people's relationship with the body goes.

However, we're becoming aware that the body does its own thinking and has its own consciousness. My body is as much 'me' as my thoughts or feelings are. The body notices and experiences things, which it passes to the mind to reflect on. Some of these things are obvious (it's cold outside today), but some are subtle and packed full of genius (my gut tells me something's wrong here). We tend to associate the mind with the head and the emotions with the heart.

But the gut has a lot to tell us, and so does the rest of the remarkable physical organism we live inside.

Our body is a big part of our memory. Whereas the mind can just replay events from the past, the body lives them. The body remembers how to do things that the mind doesn't. The body stores feelings for us. Many emotions have a physical sensation and, often, a location in the body. The body is there with us, experiencing our feelings. The body stores stresses and traumas for us, doing its best to limit their impact on our lives. We might go through a very difficult time, or experience a sudden shock or trauma. Losing somebody we love, or being involved in a car accident or some other sudden physical trauma, or suddenly losing an aspect to our lives that we loved and needed. We need to go on, we need to keep functioning, so the body does its best to help. It holds our hurt and upset, it tries to heal physical wounds, it tries to keep us safe, stable and functioning until the danger or shock passes.

What we find when we begin to explore the nature of the body is an incredibly rich ecosystem and consciousness. For many people, this journey only happens when the body has taken all that it can and begins to break down. It's held memories of trauma for decades, but it just can't go on. Now you feel pain where there hasn't ever been an injury or you find yourself unable to do things you used to do. Maybe a doctor diagnoses you with a serious condition. Maybe you just suddenly find that you have no energy at all. Your body, this remarkable friend who has been with you throughout your whole journey, is asking for your attention and your help. In a culture that's addicted to the mind, where the wisdom, awareness, consciousness and compassion of the body is all but ignored, where the body is only there to serve the needs of the mind, we can be annoyed and baffled when it doesn't do what we tell it to do. But this is an invitation to learn.

Further exploration

The best ways to explore and begin meeting the body are through physical practices. Allow your attention to leave the chatter of the mind and enter the direct physicality of the body as it moves, stretches and works. This can feel scary or embarrassing for people who are used to living in the mind. For other people who more naturally feel at home in the body, it'll be easy. Yoga is perhaps the most obvious way in. Like Buddhism, it is an ancient practice that offers many levels of learning and exploration. I certainly recommend classes over learning by yourself, but any sustained engagement with yoga will help.

Other physical practices that begin to open our awareness of the wisdom of the body include qi gong, traditional martial arts, intensive workouts like HIIT and power lifting and unconventional movement patterns like Animal Flow. Dancing of all kinds can also be a wonderful way to freely express the unique, precious organism of the body.

Be open to leaving your mind behind and connecting with everything your body is and everything it can do.

If you'd like to know more about the nature of trauma and how it's held and stored by the body, then I'd recommend a couple of books. *The Body Keeps the Score* by Bessel van der Kolk is an incredible explanation of the effects of trauma on the body and how to resolve them. I also recommend the older work of the psychotherapist, Peter Levine and his book *Waking the Tiger*. Levine talks about how humans evolved into their relationship with trauma, how common misconceptions about trauma leave people feeling powerless about it, and what action we can take to release, shift and ease the impact of physically-held trauma.

Both of these books are obviously focused on trauma, but both also convey important messages about the way the body works, how it relates to feeling and thinking, and why a good relationship with the body is so important.

The unconscious

A great deal goes on inside us that we're either semi-conscious of, or utterly unaware of. That is, it's beyond or inaccessible to our conscious mind, except in extraordinary circumstances. Our hearts beat, our cells divide, our tissues repair and our blood chemistry is carefully regulated. These things aren't within our conscious control. In the same way, we have no awareness at all of the processing that's constantly going on in our unconscious mind. We only become aware that this is going on when it pops up into our consciousness, when it triggers an expected choice of behaviour or when we say something we didn't know we were going to say. Perhaps we wake up with a brilliant answer to a problem that we've been wrestling with. Perhaps our dreams show us images and ideas that we never knew were within us. Perhaps we make a 'Freudian slip' and say a word we didn't mean to say, which shows us something important is going on under the surface. These are examples of the unconscious making brief contact with the consciousness.

The image everyone uses to describe the unconscious is a boat on a great ocean. This image has been used throughout history: it appears in the writings and poetry of ancient teachers from Greek mythology to Nordic rune lore.

The boat is conscious awareness. We can see it, we can steer it, we're aware of it. Beneath us lies the depthless and unknowable ocean, full of wonders and terrors. This is the unconscious.

Marketing executives became very interested in early research into the unconscious in the early 20th Century. They used it, and continue to use it, to manipulate us into buying their products. Our deepest needs, desires, longings, fears and hopes arise from the unconscious and if these are triggered without us realising, we buy things without noticing that we've been manipulated. Today there is a great deal of money put into things like the layout of supermarkets to ensure that we're encouraged to buy things without noticing. Our voting habits are also manipulated by combining data-mining and analysis with an understanding of the unconscious mind. Whether you know it or not, a lot of money is spent every day to manipulate you into making unconscious choices.

One reason we tend not to notice when our unconscious takes control, for example when we say something we never meant to say or when we buy something because we've been cleverly steered into buying it, is because we really want to believe that we're in control of ourselves. For people brought up in a mind-addicted culture, it can be very uncomfortable to think that conscious, rational thought only makes up a small part of who we are, and that unconscious desires and needs are having a huge impact on our decisions. When we do something that surprises us, or make a choice we don't really understand, or when we're manipulated into believing something, agreeing with something, or voting a certain way, we still want to maintain this illusion that the conscious mind is in control and calling the shots. What we'll do, in fact, is rewrite history. We'll notice something that we don't understand in our own behaviour and we'll quickly invent a reason why we wanted to do that all along. It can be tricky to notice, but if you start looking out for it you might catch yourself rewriting history to ensure you feel like you're in control.

The unconscious is a big part of who we are. It's therefore important that we know it, or at least understand its currents, tides and tempests. You will never fully explore its depths, but you can be ready for its effects. Here we begin to leave behind the familiarity of clear definitions and predictable patterns. In the world of the unconscious, intuition, association and imagery become more important that logic and rationality. Thankfully, we have inherited a tool for understanding the unconscious mind, one which we already use daily without knowing its power. Like the Buddhists devoted their attention to a study of the mind, so storytellers, saga poets and sages of the West, and especially shamanic traditions, embarked on studies of the unconscious. The famous psychologist Carl Jung made a great study of myths and their power to reveal aspects of the unconscious psyche, although it is the mythologist Joseph Campbell who stands out as the figure who restored the place of myth in the modern world as a method for personal and cultural understanding, rather than simply a form of entertainment.

Myths are stories that carry meaning. Myths are the stories that people in a culture tell one another in order to define, enshrine and renew their shared beliefs, values and priorities. Myths are written around characters who represent important aspects of the things we all believe about people. The hero in the story does what we expect heroes to do, because we all share an understanding about what a hero is. These core characters are the archetypes of our culture. A warrior is what we all know a warrior to be. A queen, a knight, a whore, a villain, a traitor, a damsel in distress, a magician or a shaman. We all know what these characters represent, feel like and mean in a story. When we simply tell the story of a trip to the shops to buy a bottle of milk, we might mention some archetypes without even realising it. Jung called this vast reservoir of shared knowledge the 'collective unconscious', a single body of knowledge that we all use to communicate profound ideas quickly and powerfully with one another.

A study of mythology is also a study of the unconscious. Older and more mature cultures used stories of the underworld, of great quests, of the gods, angels and daemons that guide our steps. Our unconscious is full of needs, drives and fears. It's a restless ocean that we can only learn about from its effects on our lives and the myths that we've told about ourselves over the millennia. Our individual unconsciousness uses myth to communicate with us. Our dreams are often made up of characters that represent aspects of ourselves, or important people (or our beliefs about important people) from our lives. It communicates with us by guiding our choices to meet our unconscious needs and excise our shadow-self (both needs and shadow are explored below).

The important thing to take from the nature of the unconscious is that it is vast, and inaccessible, and mysterious. It is, however, hugely relevant to our daily lives. The idea that the world is a rational and ordered place and that humans should strive to be rational and ordered people is the delusion of a mind-addicted culture. We can be in control of ourselves and we have ultimate responsibility for our actions. That is one of the core messages of this book. But we'll know ourselves better, and therefore have more control and power in our lives, if we understand that a huge and important aspect of us is bound up in mystery, intuition and instinct. It's necessary for anybody who wants to truly know themselves to relinquish comforting ideas of straight lines and logic and be open to mystery and wonder. The unconscious mind will pop up unexpectedly and deliver important, often brilliant or revelatory news at any time. That is normal. That is humanity.

Further exploration

To begin really understanding the hidden meaning in the myths and stories from ancient to modern time, and their relationship to human consciousness, I recommend a couple of fantastic resources.

The classic in the field of mythology is *The Hero with a Thousand Faces* by Joseph Campbell. I'll talk about Campbell more later, but he was one of the great students of worldwide myths in the precious time after global travel became accessible, but before our single, dominant culture stamped out older, land-based cultures around the world. He collated the great stories of different peoples and, looking at them altogether and working with some of the great psychologists and sociologists of his time, he came to see the common threads and the important messages that they hold for all people.

Stan Groff also explores this idea in *The Cosmic Game*.

Finally, there is a type of psychotherapy called Shadow Work which makes extensive use of messages and language from our unconscious self. If you'd like to know more, researching and engaging with Shadow Work and can be helpful. I'll return to the Shadow later in this chapter.

Spirit

In my experience, human beings tend to have yearnings to encounter an aspect of themselves which seems to go beyond the individual and transcend the ordinary. In the Christian tradition, which has influenced our culture so much, there's the idea that a part of God resides within us. Other traditions echo this, providing a framework for the individual to find divinity within themselves, while allowing for the flawed and temporal nature of the rest of the self. Some suggest that our soul is interwoven with the soul of the world so that individuality and personal identity become irrelevant and all beings become one. Some make us the children of gods. Some make us aspects of a single universal consciousness which has broken itself into many pieces to understand its own nature by experiencing separation and unique, individual perspectives. For some of us, simply being in nature, in a calm and open way, brings us a kind of peace and understanding that transcends our thought and conscious knowledge.

Today it's very hard to explore spiritual experience without either falling into the reductive, anti-religious dogma of the mind-addicted culture, or being absorbed by a religion of faith that brings a lot of extra baggage. But in between these two, and separate from both, is a rich and important seam for all of us to explore. I encourage you to be both curious and rigorous in your approach. Spirit is not entertainment, it is not escapism, it is not an emotion and it is not a thought. It is something else, and it's there for you to explore in your own way.

Further exploration

If a religious or spiritual tradition calls to you, feel free to follow that. I simply urge you not to get lost in bliss or in the reassurance of sharing a belief with others. These things are wonderful feelings, but will ultimately hold back your spiritual growth. I talk more about the pitfalls that can snare the unwary traveller in book 3 of this series.

If no clear path exists for you, make time to explore different traditions. I would suggest at least one of the popular Abrahamic traditions (Christianity, Islam or Judaism), some time praying and spinning with the sufis, some time drumming and dancing with the shamans, some time in contemplation with Buddhists and some time in the wild vibrancy of a living polytheistic faith like those found in India.

Beware of charlatans. A scepticism and a slowness to trust will help keep your spiritual thirst from being used against you. But when you encounter Grace, allow it to teach you about yourself.

The Four Directions

In the traditions of some Native American peoples, the Four Directions are a model for the nature of reality and the nature of self. In people, the Four Directions are: **Mind**, **Emotion**, **Body** and **Spirit**.

We each feel more confident or comfortable with some of these aspects than others. Some of us are physical first, tending to be practical and confident with physical expression, but perhaps less comfortable with rigorous mental work or honest and vulnerable emotional expression. Others are naturally strong in Emotion, but less so in Body or Spirit.

Where are you most comfortable?

In order to find balance in your life, you will need to pay attention to all four Directions.

Needs

Intrinsic needs are baked into our DNA. They reside in the unconscious, the body and the emotions, and they have a profound and direct effect on us every day.

Needs are things that are essential to be happy, healthy and whole. They are essential and undeniable. Each need requires one or more things in order to be fulfilled. An unfulfilled need becomes a problem, and the longer it goes unmet, the more insistent it becomes. Needs will find a way to be fulfilled if we do not provide them with the thing they demand from us. They cannot be suppressed forever, but we can choose the way that we meet a need.

We may feel a need for food. If we're used to a diet of sugary or processed foods, we'll tend to meet this need that way. But the need for food can be met just as well by eating fresh fruit and vegetables, by having a balanced and healthy diet. It might take a while for your need to understand that it's being properly met in a new way, but as long as the core need is being fulfilled then it will calm down. If you find that your need for sugar continues then you'll need to widen your enquiry. Was it really a need for food at all? Was it the need for something else?

However, if we're hungry and we don't eat, then this intrinsic need will pop up in unexpected parts of our lives. We might become angry or upset. We might become fixated on thoughts of food. We might make a series of strange choices that sabotage whatever we're trying to do, so that we stop doing it and eat instead.

Needs that are not fulfilled will find ways to manipulate or sabotage our behaviour so they become fulfilled. This isn't because they're mean or evil: every need is trying to keep you safe from something and it's working to protect you. Needs are all part of your highest good.

Some of our mental and emotional needs will be the kind of thing we expect: needs for love, acceptance, safety, belonging, expression, recognition and fulfilment. Others will be things we might want to pretend don't exist. For example, if you're a very independent person then you might not feel comfortable with your intrinsic needs for love and belonging.

Intrinsic needs versus Adaptations

If you feel a need for something that's unhealthy, or unkind, or doesn't serve your highest good, then you're not looking at an intrinsic need, you're looking at a way you have adapted to an unmet need at some point in your life. Often these adaptations happen in our childhood.

Some people have a need for control, for example. Their friends would call them a 'control freak'. They might harm themselves or others out of their need for control. However, the need for control is an unhealthy adaptation to deeper needs. In this case, it's probably the need for safety. You may simply have learned that in order to feel safe, you have to control things, and so we mislabel the need for safety as the need for control.

Our intrinsic needs, as explored and named by the famous psychotherapist Abram Maslow, are all directed towards our healing and thriving. I'll be covering these in more detail in book 2. Needs like control, or domination, or power, or predictability, are adaptations to try to meet a deeper need. In this case, it's usually the need for safety. The need for exciting or edgy sex tends, in reality, to be the needs for connection, intimacy and, recognition and spiritual expression. A need to 'act up', be dramatic or a need for attention tends to be the need for belonging. We can easily fail to recognise the root need, and instead believe that our adaptation is the need itself.

To add further complexity, many of these needs will be unwelcome, or might manifest as things that cause embarrassment or shame. These parts of ourselves are called our Shadow. The unconscious is not bound by the rules of civilised behaviour or morality, but we are. If you notice a deep and forceful need for something that's unwanted or unwelcome, you will need to find a way to allow it to be met, or some way to manage it. If you don't, your unconscious needs will manipulate your behaviour to do things that you may not expect and may not be able to fully control.

Over time, we can come to understand our needs more deeply. If we understand that a need has arisen from an early-life experience, for example, and we do the necessary healing and personal development to remove the power this event has over us, we'll find that the need becomes less imperative or vanishes altogether. Sometimes simply understanding the root of a need is enough to break its hold over us. Sadly, most people never do this work and refuse to admit that unconscious needs even exist. They remain victims of their own inner processes and never take back true control of themselves.

Further exploration

We'll look at needs more fully in book 2. Some of the exploration needed is private, while some of it is best done with a therapist or in groups. You can probably name many of your core needs right now, but others might take a little digging to realise. You might need to ask people who know you well what they think you need from life, and which core needs most strongly drive your choices and behaviour.

Toxic Shame and the origin of Masks

Toxic shame is something that's become so normal, so everyday and common, that we hardly ever notice it. It's one of the foundation pillars of our culture and it's the basis for many of our beliefs, expectations and the way we relate to ourselves and to other people. There are entire schools of psychology that study the ways that we interact with each other, based on toxic shame. We are taught to expect and accept toxic shame in our early childhoods, and we continue to use it and allow it through our entire lives. It begins with the way that our parents treat us, and the behaviour we witness in them. Mum and dad also grew up with toxic shame, and passed it on to us without realising. If you, as a little child, did something wrong then a parent who is psychologically and emotionally skilled, aware and present will respond by stopping you, laying down clear boundaries and, where appropriate, explaining why something is wrong. But in a world where our parents have little or no psycho-spiritual education and where they are exhausted, confused, depleted or overwhelmed, they will tend to use toxic shame to control our behaviour.

It might manifest as a total overreaction to a situation. A child cries or throws a tantrum in a supermarket or other public place, and the mortified, embarrassed parent screams at their child. Or it might be a response of disgust or contempt to something the child has done wrong. 'How could you be so stupid?' 'That's disgusting, don't ever do that again!' 'How dare you behave like that?'

The parent is saying more than 'you've done something wrong'. They are throwing enormous emotional weight behind the statement. They are dumping shame, judgement, rage, or their own fears onto a vulnerable child. The experience for the child is that their behaviour has caused the parent to suddenly and violently withdraw their love. Parents, to young children, are giant figures of care and love. The child knows they utterly depend on the parent and they use the parent as a template for how to act, how to know right and wrong, how to be a person. To find that love is no longer available is one of the most terrifying experiences for a young child. The child quickly learns the terror of rejection and the withdrawal of love. They learn that their safety and security are at stake if they get certain things wrong. This lesson is reinforced as they grow up by peers, teachers and role models. What we're left with is a clear pattern of things that we want or need, but which trigger this shaming response in others.

When we internalise this pattern, we're left with a story that goes: there is something intrinsically wrong with me, and if people really see who I am they would reject me and nobody would love me. This belief is really, really common in our culture. It says that deep down we're basically unworthy of love. It's a kind of stagnant, unchanging, unquestioned and paralysing shame. It is the shame of being the person we believe ourselves to be, the person we've learned that we need to keep hidden. This belief sits somewhere between consciousness and unconscious. We can be aware of its effects, and if we focus on it we can realise that we know this feeling pretty well, but the feeling slips beneath the surface of the great ocean of the unconscious and has all sorts of unexpected or unintended effects on our choices, words and actions.

Toxic shame goes on to dictate our relationships. If we believe on some level that we're basically a bad person, basically unworthy of love, then our mission in life becomes developing a mask that is so attractive, lovable, impressive and complete that we will never experience the pain of rejection. People will say 'wow, what a great person!' Our society can be seen as one great competition to make the best mask. There are prizes for making a better, more convincing mask that shows all the things we think we're supposed to be. We get rewarded with good jobs that pay well, with expensive things that prove to other people how good we are. Most importantly, we are rewarded with love. Many friendships and intimate relationships in our culture are between the masks of two people, with those people never truly meeting, even in a life-long relationship.

Brené Brown, author, researcher and public speaker, who has delivered some of the most popular talks on TED.com, has studied and written extensively about shame, its effects on our behaviour, and how to overcome it. Vulnerability, she says, is the antidote to shame. As long as we keep living behind a mask in order to protect ourselves from imagined rejection, we'll never truly connect with others. According to Brené, we are "hardwired for connection". It is the thing that we most treasure and most need in our lives. If we have a belief that we should feel ashamed of ourselves, we will not truly connect with another human being. We won't let them in. So Brené explores the skills necessary to lower the mask, step into our lives with vulnerability and learn to endure the feelings of exposure and the fear of rejection.

These skills have the power to transform our personal lives and, ultimately, transform the way we function as a society.

Where Brené talks about shame, I talk about toxic shame. As we'll explore later in this book, it's been my experience that some shame is completely right and appropriate. Adult shame, where we recognise our own harmful behaviour and choices, can be a healthy and proper way to restore our behaviour to something we can feel rightfully proud of. The function of a healthy shame is to alert us to choices that breach our own beliefs of right and wrong. That's the emotion doing its job properly. But this persistent shame that lies beneath our beliefs about ourselves and our relationships isn't helpful to our personal growth and serves no good purpose. It's the remnant of the response by a child who didn't know how to do better. It lurks behind our friendships, our sex lives, our parenting, our shopping and voting habits and our aspirations for ourselves, to name just a few things. It's pernicious, ongoing and does us a lot of harm.

Further exploration

Brené Brown's work is exceptional in helping you to understand the nature of toxic shame, to identify how it's shaped your life and influenced your choices, and how to begin developing skills in vulnerability to break the hold that toxic shame has over your life. If you found yourself resonating with my description of toxic shame, I urge you to engage with Brené's work. Her book *Daring Greatly* is an excellent place to begin.

If you're curious about the ways that toxic shame has subtly shaped the way we relate to one another, you might enjoy learning about a field of psychology called Transactional Analysis. This field studies the individual 'transactions' that go on between people when they're communicating. I say something to you, hopeful to get a certain response (maybe approval or sympathy) and if you respond in the way I expect then we both feel good. A kind of transaction has happened between us.

A certain model in Transactional Analysis which looks at the three most common masks we wear to gain approval and a safe kind of identity, called the Karpman Drama Triangle, has become a big part of the work I do with my coaching clients and I'll be exploring it later in this series.

Shadow

The term 'shadow' was first coined by Carl Jung. Just as there are things that we're proud of about ourselves, that we are happy for people to know about us, there are parts of us that are secret, dark and hidden. We prefer to pretend that these parts of us don't exist. Our darker impulses, our secret desires, our longings for things that aren't ok or acceptable. The things that we feel ashamed of, the things we don't like about ourselves. You know something is part of your inner shadow if you notice yourself pushing it to the edges of your conscious awareness, or if you try to ignore or avoid it because you feel shame, discomfort, embarrassment, fear or disgust about it. We keep these things out of the light of our everyday selves and we push them to lurk somewhere at the periphery, suppressed, barely noticed, associated with darkness.

Things that reside in the shadow tend to have a strong hold over our imagination. Horror movies terrify and excite us because they show us the dark things inside ourselves. Taboos and sexual fetishes exist because we are both excited and repelled by aspects of ourselves that we keep hidden. The revulsion and the excitement feed on one another, leaving us with a potent mix of fascinating feelings.

This series of books is about empowerment through understanding. It's a guidebook to your inner and outer journey towards a life that's fulfilling, nourishing and under control. But there are parts of you that want to do things that you can't be proud of, things that want to sabotage your good choices.

The most common way that we lose control is by denying the presence of something that is manipulating or influencing us. Every time we deny and reject something, or pretend it doesn't exist because it seems so unacceptable that we don't know how to deal with it, we reinforce its power over us. So it's important that you factor your shadow self into your journey of awakening. The shadow is there, in everybody. It is your fears, your loathings, your shames, your hidden longings.

A parable from Native American teachers is useful here, one that was passed on to me by Mac Macartney, who spent 20 years studying with indigenous people in North America. They call these dark impulses the 'wild dogs'. Imagine you are sitting on an open plain at night. You've built a fire and you're staring into the flames, but out in the darkness you can hear wild dogs howling, barking and yapping. They sound huge and terrible and you fear them, so you huddle closer to the fire. But what happens if you welcome the wild dogs into your firelight? Now you can see them, and perhaps you begin to realise that they aren't so great and terrible after all. Out in the unknown darkness things can sound far worse than they are. As long as we keep things squashed, hidden or pushed away they exert great control over us. But if we welcome them into the light and begin to get to know them, we begin to break their hold over us.

This isn't the same as giving them free rein. This isn't about letting all our darkest impulses loose. Control is a big part of the message of this book. Rather, this is about acceptance and awareness, so you can make good choices in full knowledge of who you are and what needs you have.

This book will offer you signposts towards a certain kind of life, and in that life you will be strong, empowered and you will make good choices. We do not allow our shadow selves to rule our lives, sabotaging our great ambitions, stifling our imagination, or making us ruin friendships, relationships or opportunities. Left unchecked, our shadow would have us hurting people, betraying trust and causing harm in the world. Indeed, that is what humanity is doing on a large scale. We have lost our ability to welcome our wild dogs in from the darkness and learn about our greatest fears – and in so doing, we have lost the ability to make consistent, good choices.

Further exploration

Books, websites and courses exist for those who want to understand and explore their own shadow. If you feel that you could do with a better relationship with your shadow, I would recommend looking for a workshop or course where a teacher will guide you through this challenging and sometimes savage experience into the inner dark. You might find things there that are deeply unsettling, so I only recommend you study this alone if you feel you'll be ok doing so.

One online resource I can recommend is exploringtheshadow.co.uk by Shadow-work expert Marianne Hill. Many of Marianne's blog entries are excellent, clear ways to understand this murky but vitally important side of the human psyche.

Some good books on this topic are:

A Little Book on the Human Shadow by Robert Bly and William Booth

Meeting the Shadow: Hidden Power of the Dark Side of Human Nature by Connie Zweig

Dark Side of the Light Chasers: Reclaiming your power, creativity, brilliance, and dreams by Debbie Ford

Wounds

I'll refer to wounds throughout this book, so I will say a few words about what I mean.

Life is not always smooth. When we are very young, we are at our most vulnerable and we can be hurt in ways that aren't always visible. We pick up psycho-spiritual scars from traumatic events that happen to us or sustained neglect of some kind. We learn bad lessons that stifle our growth or which make us repeat self-harmful patterns of behaviour. Most commonly this comes from our parents because we trusted them as our care-givers, role models and teachers. For the infant, the primary care-giver (usually mum) is god. But lots of other things can wound us. Growing up with injustice, prejudice or social inequality. Bullying or harassment at school. A violent or traumatic event that leaves a physical or psycho-spiritual wound.

In a forest, few trees grow straight and true. Most will have notches on their bark, kinks in their trunks. Sometimes we see trees that have been smashed, cracked or burned and they've continued to grow around the wounds. It's the same with people. Some wounds are physical, or have obvious effects. Others are carried in the heart and the mind and continue to influence us for years afterwards.

Many wounds can be healed. Probably more than you think. This is one of the main functions of counselling, psychotherapy and psychiatry. These professions exist, in part, to help us understand, explore, process and heal wounds that we carry in our minds and in our hearts. The body gets involved in all of our mental and emotional wounds, so it too will require healing even if you didn't seem to take any physical harm. I have been lucky enough to learn about Upledger CranioSacral Therapy, which is effective at healing and releasing physically-held traumas, but a range of other physical therapies exist, from the many forms of massage to things like Shiatsu and the Alexander Technique. Part of your personal journey of awakening and empowerment may involve sampling these forms of therapy to find the one that supports you best.

Sadly, in my experience, some wounds cannot be healed in a conscious way or in a predictable time-frame, because they are too deep, or were caused too early in our lives, or because we simply hold on to them too tightly. Some wounds may take a very long time to shift even a little bit. So there are wounds we carry that we must learn to compensate for, in the way that a hurt leg is compensated with a walking stick. We learn how these wounds affect us, and we make allowances for them. Our friends or partners know about them and they adapt and forgive us because they love us. When we're overwhelmed by anxiety or fear or depression or anything else that arises from a wound we carry, it's understood. When we enter into relationships, we hope that our wounds will be accepted and eventually cherished by our partners.

But you may be surprised what can change, what can be healed. I encourage you to be open to the possibility that you may find ways to heal things about yourself that are old and seem impossible to change.

Like a notched or gnarled tree, our growth can be stunted by an old wound. The act of seeking help to heal our wounds is a profound act of self-love. It is also an act of love to those who depend on us and who care about us. Some of us tend to sit in the knowledge of our wounds, fixating on them, sure that we'll never get over them. But love is a tremendously healing thing, and as we'll explore later in this book, loving yourself in an active and committed way is one of the most important skills we all need to develop. Love opens the possibility of healing and change, and it inspires us to seek out healing when we need it.

Further exploration

Do you know your wounds? Do you know the knocks and bruises that sometimes send you off-course, and do you know the core wounds that have dictated the course of your life and defined your story?

Reflection, such as regular journaling, is an excellent way to meet and identify your wounds, and sometimes it's just your attention and your compassion that will allow them to shift and fade.

At other times, it's important to seek out professional support. Counsellors and psychotherapists are now pretty common and you'll find one near you. Investing in this is an investment in yourself and the person you might become if you could heal this part of yourself and grow beyond it. Physical therapists are also increasingly common and can be very supportive in making breakthroughs in your personal healing.

Will

The force that your mind, unconscious and emotions create is called the will. People also called it willpower. You need will to push through anything difficult, to compel anything to happen. Every time there is an opposing force, but you want to make progress, you need to apply a greater force, so if you want to achieve something in your life, anything at all, your will has to be stronger than any barriers, resistance or distractions that stand between you and that thing.

Every time your thoughts or feelings become action, you are exerting your will. Everything from telling your arm to move, to making yourself say difficult words to your partner, to resisting that pudding. Will is the conduit between conceptualisation and reality. Without will, we are trapped withing our imagination, unable to make our ideas become reality.

Generally we don't notice our will, and generally this is fine. You're using it all the time. You use your will when you push yourself out of the cosy bed in the morning. You're gathering your will when you're preparing to do something difficult. A gym routine, or a job application, or a healthy dinner is all driven by your will.

If there is any kind of opposing force, your will must be stronger. You need to hit the gym? The forces pushing against you might be external (you don't have much time, or travelling to the gym is difficult, or someone else wants your time and attention) or they might be internal (your discomfort with your body, your anxiety about being in the gym, the fact that it's quite nice to just sit around at home). If you're going to make it to the gym, your will is going to need to be stronger than all the forces acting against you.

If you want a promotion at work, or to ask that person out on a date, or to tell an old friend a difficult truth, you will immediately be facing a bunch of forces that are working to stop you taking that step. Your will must be greater than those forces.

We tend to know people who seem to have stronger or weaker wills. Strong-willed people stick to good routines, or make themselves do difficult things, or take bigger risks. People who are weak-willed tend to follow along with others, struggle to get things done and often feel trapped in their lives.

The important thing to understand about will is that it isn't fixed. You will usually enter adulthood with a certain amount of willpower. Your early life education will have taught you certain ways to handle your challenges, and this includes how to develop and focus will. But will is like a muscle. With practice it grows, becomes stronger, and no matter who you are, you can become somebody with formidable willpower. I have seen timid, quiet people who never rocked the boat and always struggled to be heard, become people who made uncomfortable conversations happens, focused on difficult projects and overcame persistent old problems in their thinking or emotions.

Willpower isn't, ultimately, enough. You can't force everything to happen, and you can't keep pushing forever. Most of this series of books is about growing beyond your challenges rather than continuing to push against them. But there will always be times, no matter how far your journey takes you, that are difficult and require you to push your way through.

So I would encourage you to treat your willpower like a muscle and develop it accordingly. Begin doing difficult things on purpose. Have that conversation. Put yourself forwards for that exam. Push yourself to the next level. Challenge yourself. You may gain all sorts of things along the way, but you will also develop a strong will at the same time.

Further exploration

Any book about achievement and smashing goals will help you here. So books like *Unlimited Power* by Antony Robbins or *The Way of the SEAL* by Mark Divine are great companions at becoming someone who is more effective and focused, more skilled at developing and deploying their will.

The 'I'

I've mentioned the four directions of the human person: mind, emotions, body and spirit. We have talked about the vast ocean of the unconscious, the needs that drive us, the toxic shame that suffuses our culture, the inner shadow that we all carry and the wounds that can influence our choices.

If we take all that away, if we remove the babble of the mind, the flow of emotions, the unique consciousness of the body, the inner spark of the spirit and all the other things, what do we have left?

We have a thing that simply is. We have a core of awareness, always present, never distracted. This part of us does not change, doesn't grow or get hurt, doesn't exist in the past or the future(because these are constructs of the mind). I refer to this part of us simply as the 'I'. When we deeply meditate and the mind and all other distractions fall away and we simply are, we have returned to the 'I'. We are born with this awareness and it is with us until we die. It cannot be harmed by traumatic events, and this perfectly detached part of us can be a consolation in difficult times.

In my experience, love is the natural state of life. Love is not an emotion, it is a natural and true way of being where our minds are quiet, our emotions flow naturally, we act with compassion and care and we are fully present in a moment. Two people sharing love have returned to the natural state that we inhabit before we learn all of the complicated and messy business that life requires of us.

The 'I', which never has to deal with the complicated and messy business of life, exists in love. It offers compassion to us and to the world.

In my experience, the 'I' is a hugely reassuring and comforting presence. When things are hard, or overwhelming, or lead us away from ourselves, the 'I' is always there, compassionately detached. A core part of our identity from which we observe the world. We can't live there because the 'I' can't do relationships, can't do anything, but it is a part of us, the true self, the centre of our consciousness, to which we can always return and find stillness.

Further exploration

Meditation is a necessary part of developing a relationship with your 'I', as you'll need to quieten and calm everything else to begin to notice it.

Beyond that, I simply invite you to be curious and aware of this aspect of self. It requires a stillness of being to notice and experience, but the unchanging continuity of the 'I' may be profoundly helpful at difficult times of your life.

How esteem shapes your life

In the next book in this trilogy, we're going to dive into the detail of how to build a consistently happy, successful, satisfying life. I'm going to ask you to consider taking conscious, active control of all your choices and responses, to restore your power to create an amazing life. This is the first of the 12 Rules. I'm also going to ask you to recognise that you have fundamental, unavoidable human needs. That's the second Rule. According to the best research, we all share this set of intrinsic needs, and I'll be covering this in detail in book 2. However, I'm going to talk about one of them now because it's important you understand it now.

What is esteem?

Here's a definition of esteem from the Chambers dictionary:

esteem verb *(esteemed, esteeming)*

1 to value, respect or think highly of someone or something.

2 formal to consider someone to be a specified thing.

noun high regard or respect.

ETYMOLOGY: 15c: from French estimer, from Latin aestimare to estimate the value of something.

Esteem is a strangely universal aspect of human thinking. It's one of our intrinsic needs. We can find examples of the search for esteem in the oldest stories, in different indigenous cultures around the world, and between modern social groups. Everyone seems to carry this instinct to measure themselves and their worth, and to measure everyone around them, and thus to deduce a value for themselves or a place for themselves in some kind of social pecking order. I don't think I've ever known anyone, even the most enlightened or apparently evolved, who does not measure self-worth and the worth of others in some way.

Esteem is the respect and recognition we give to other people when they're doing well on this scale, or the judgement we feel for people who are failing on our scale. Self-esteem is the feelings of pride and emotional security we give ourselves when we consider ourselves to be doing well on our own scales.

We each measure esteem in different ways. Conflicts between people are often because they have different measures of esteem, different criteria for success and worth, or they assign respect based on different things.

How do we measure esteem?

I've made a point of spending time with all sorts of people from all sorts of backgrounds. I guess it's a point of pride for me. I've spent an unusual amount of time with millionaires and outwardly successful executives and business leaders. I've spent at least as long with homeless people and convicts. I have made a point of getting to know artists and stay-at-home parents and religious leaders and activists and academics of all kinds.

Everyone measures esteem in different ways, and in general they don't notice they're doing this, and in general they unconsciously assume that everyone else must measure esteem in the same way they do. But no matter how attached you might be to your way of assessing esteem and worth, there's no objectively correct way. Everyone believes that certain properties of people make them better or worse, more valuable or less valuable, more important or less important, more worth listening to and emulating or less. It's part of someone's belief structure, and often its inherited from parents, teachers, peers of mentors.

As a coach, I tend to get a fairly high amount of respect from people. And yet, there are always new clients who treat me casually, or with disdain, in their first few sessions. For these people, I might have skills they need, but I don't measure up on their criteria for esteem and worth. I'm not particularly rich, I'm not powerful, I don't drive an expensive car, I don't make multi-million pound decisions every day. I'm just another professional they're hiring, like a plumber or a locksmith. This tends to shift quickly, because people's measures of esteem quickly shift when they engage in transformational personal development work. Once you've explained your fears to someone, or told them your dreams, or cried in front of them, or talked to them about your grief at the death of your mother, you tend to stop measuring their worth in conventional ways.

Here are some common ways that people assess someone's worth, and assign them esteem:

- Rich people are better than poor people.
- If this is how you measure esteem then you will tend to respect rich people more than poor people, and you will base your own self-worth on your income and wealth. You might make the unconscious assumption that rich people must be rich for good reasons, like they're smarter or harder working; while poor people might be stupid or lazy.
- People who wear the correct brands of clothes, or drive the right cars, are better.
- If you measure esteem this way, you will immediately notice what people are wearing or what car they drive, and you will

put someone on a spectrum of worth based on what brands you notice.

• Thin people are better than fat people.

• You are highly conscious of your own body shape and you assign more value to people who are thin than those who are fat.

• Fame, glory or renown.

• If you value these things highly, then the ability to draw a crowd to an event, or be recognised by people you've never met, are badges of success and esteem.

• Goodness and moral character.

• Somebody's choices tell you everything you need to know about them. Is a person generous, kind, caring and decent? Then that person has you respect and you would rank them as being a more valuable person than someone who is selfish, self-oriented, unkind or deceitful.

• Adherence to laws, or religious tenets.

• If this is how you measure esteem, you admire those who most closely follow the 'correct' guidelines.

• Technical skill, niche information l or progress through a career path.

• You derive your self-worth through your abilities in your chosen field and you rank highly those who know as much or more than you.

- Skin colour.

- Here, you rank some ethnicities higher than others. This doesn't necessarily mean that you see yourself as the ideal 'type'. I've worked with plenty of clients who, sadly, felt shame or inferiority because of their skin colour.

- Sexual orientation or gender identification.

- Again, you see some people here are intrinsically better than others, and you rank yourself accordingly.

- Political activism.

- You would assign more value to people who agree with your political views than those who disagree, and the elite are those who are politically active on behalf of your political party or view.

So we carry a range of measures of esteem in our heads. We usually have several of them, but some matter more to use than others. We might not always admit to ourselves that some of them are so important to us. It's quite possible to believe that we measure someone's worth in one way, but actually we're measuring it in another way that we don't want to acknowledge. For example if we feel ashamed of our way of measuring the value of ourselves and others.

Broadly, the way this works in people's minds is this:

1. I believe that THESE THINGS (whatever your measures of esteem are) are the proper way to assess somebody's worth

2. If I have a lot of those things, then I am a good/worthy/ successful person. I feel esteem, which means that I feel good about myself and I feel confident of where I exist on my social spectrum.

   For example, if I measure someone's worth and assign someone esteem because of their wealth, then rank myself very highly if I have a lot of wealth. I'll compare myself to others based on their wealth, putting myself above poorer people and below richer people.

3. I am better than those with less of my chosen measurement. This quickly begins to feel like moral superiority. For example, I have a lot of money so I am wiser and intrinsically *better* than a poor person.

4. I am inferior to those who have more of my chosen measurement. I should listen to them and try to become more like them.

Why measures of esteem matter so much

People behave differently, depending on how well they measure up on their own personal scales. Those who rate themselves as doing well tend to walk tall and proud, sure of themselves and their superiority to people around them. Meanwhile, people punish themselves and loathe themselves if, in their belief structure, they aren't measuring up.

We seem to need this thing. We seem to need to find a way that we are comfortable to measure the worth of a human person, either ourselves or others. But I would say that some measures are more authentic than others, and certainly some leave you much more vulnerable to manipulation and emotional crises than others.

The effects of these belief structures on our lives are truly phenomenal. They change so many of the things that matter.

We will choose the type of relationship we have, the people we want in our lives, and the ways we communicate based on our unconsciously beliefs about what has value and what doesn't. This will hugely affect how our needs for belonging, recognition, security, stimulation and love are satisfied, and this in turn will determine our mental wellbeing.

We will choose our work, and the way we behave at work, and the level of success we achieve based on our measures of worth, and thus another huge set of intrinsic needs are satisfied or frustrated by this belief structure.

Our self-esteem will be healthy, strong and robust if our measures of esteem are consistent with our personal needs, and it will be fragile, dependent and inconsistent if it doesn't.

Self-esteem

If you believe that you're doing well in life, in whatever way you measure "doing well" then you will feel good about yourself. We assign ourselves self-esteem when we compare ourselves to our own measures of worth and find we're doing well, and self-esteem has a tremendous impact on well-being, confidence, decision-making, performance and happiness.

I might believe that I'm a good person because I've been really successful. I might judge myself as bad or failing person if I've failed financially. This tells me that my measure of worth is financially-driven, and as long as I measure worth in this way, my self-esteem will be directly linked to my bank balance, my personal wealth and my financial success.

Equally, if I carry a belief that good character and moral decision-making are important then I will assign myself high self-esteem based on this. If I do something that breaks my moral code then I will feel shame and regret and it will impact my self-esteem.

This is all about beliefs. It's not about anything else. There is no objective, independent measure of a person's worth. There is only what you believe and how closely you're aligned with your own beliefs.

Self-esteem itself is our judgement about our worth as a human being. It's important for us to know that we're worthy. Again, it's an intrinsic human need. The most important things in our lives are, at their root, things like connection, safety, identity and wellness, and things like this are dependent on self-esteem. If you don't rate yourself very highly as a person then you'll tend to have low confidence, you'll struggle to be consistently effective, and you'll have higher incidence of various health problems.

And it's important to understand that you are in control of your self-esteem, and the way you assign esteem to others. The way you measure somebody's worth can change. Ideally, it should be things you've chosen rather than things you've had synthetically implanted in you by your parents, your peers or your society.

Living someone else's life

So many people move through life, unconsciously (or semi-consciously) assessing their own worth and the worth of others. They carry an elaborate belief structure about a proper way to measure this, and their belief structure has a big impact on the shape of their lives.

But people are broken into two distinct groups...

- Those who understand all this, who have investigated and explored their belief structures around worth and value, and who have updated their measures to match the things that they, personally, believe.

- Those who move through life in an unconscious way, judging themselves and others based on received wisdom.

It's entirely possible to live someone else's life. We might spend our whole lives trying, unconsciously, to earn our parents' approval by living up to their beliefs. Most likely those beliefs were also unconscious and received, so they won't match up with reality and may be entirely dysfunctional. We expect things in relationships that are both unreasonable *and aren't what we really want.* We spend decades working away in a career that makes us miserable because our unconscious impulses tell us that this is right and proper.

Other people don't have any interest in their parents' ideas, but they try to live up to someone else's belief structures. A teacher from school who made a huge impression. A celebrity or famous and charismatic leader. Your first boss who told you exactly how to live your life.

I regularly sit with clients as they hit the terrible, heart-breaking realisation that they have wasted their entire lives. It's a normal, and common, and horrible aspect of my work. They are shaken. They rage, they cry, they stare off into space, trying to process the enormity of all the wasted months, years, opportunities, connections…that they could have pursued, but didn't.

As I've already mentioned, the next book in this series will focus heavily on restoring your power and potential by encouraging you to take conscious, active control of every aspect of your life and yourself. But before we really dive into that, I wanted to bring up this enormous topic because conscious choice here makes a big difference to everything else.

What do you really value? What really matters to you? Are your beliefs your own, or did you adopt the beliefs of others because they seemed so sure about things?

This is the time to begin considering questions like this. I would rather you didn't have the realisation, towards the end of your life, that you've been prioritising things based on things you don't really believe.

Questioning and re-assessing your measures of esteem

Almost everybody is carrying other people's measures of esteem, and it takes time to notice them inside you, and even longer to begin replacing them. The important thing is to begin with the intention to free yourself from other people's expectations. It will reshape so many things if you are using your own, authentic judgements as your move through your life.

Begin by wondering what your early life taught you. What was important to your parents or guardians? What were the unspoken assumptions in your school? What did your friends value most while you were growing up?

Think about the people and organisations that have shaped you as an adult, too. Who stands out? Who have you been most affected by?

It can help to write a list of the people who moulded you. This can be an inspiring grandparent who taught you important lessons about life, or a scary boss who left scars on your thoughts and emotions. Abusive partners. Teachers who really made a difference. Authors who inspired you. Characters from TV shows who, if you're really honest with yourself, have shaped the way you handle certain situations.

Each of these people had measures for esteem. Each of them would say "this is what's best in people, and this is what's worst". Write out these two lists, for each person you've thought of.

Now you should have a big list of "positive" qualities in people, and a big list of "negative" qualities. Go through these lists and look for beliefs that you have internalised. Which of these measures have you taken on board, so that they shape your decision making, your relationships or the way you judge yourself at succeeding or failing? Maybe number each of your big lists of beliefs from 1 to 5, where 5 are those beliefs that strongly influence you to this day.

Those are your received beliefs. Those are the beliefs that have been implanted into you by others. Some of them might be wholesome and helpful and you feel good about them. Others are nonsense, or harmful, or don't fit with the person you want to be.

From there, your job is to notice, as you go about your day, which beliefs are shaping your decisions, or the words you use with people, or the kinds of conversations you have, or the harmful things you tolerate, or the positive opportunities you pass up, or the way you talk to yourself inside your head.

Be curious, be determined. Progressively notice what's going on.

And, when you feel ready to remove one of them, make that decision and then begin shifting your behaviour and language so that it doesn't show up any more.

Committing to the Journey

"News of your insignificance has been greatly exaggerated. Might you consider another possibility: that you are needed?" – Stephen Jenkinson

My belief is that there is a true self within each of us, a person who waits, buried under layers of habit, adaptation, wounds and confusion. When we recover this self, we also find radical new solutions to our challenges and we begin navigating our lives with resilience, power and grace.

In my experience, this true adult self always has certain properties. I've sat in clinics and offices and sometimes in natural surroundings, and I've watched hundreds of people meet themselves, and be excited by what's waiting for them. This self is strong, because it doesn't immediately react to triggers and knows what it wants and what it believes. It is vitally alive, deeply present in the moment and possessed of great potential to create, because it has full access to all its faculties and capacities without needing to pretend to be anything, or play small, or be what other people want it to be. This person is ready to connect deeply with others, because it can empathise with others and feel what they feel, while its strong boundaries allow her or him to not get lost in other people's experience. This self experiences the full flow of emotions, recognising them all as valid and valuable, without fear of getting stuck on just one. It is able and eager to be a positive force for others: for friends, lovers, colleagues and for the wider world.

This self is within you right now. If you haven't started your journey yet, it'll be whispering to you.

"Come home," it says, "see through the illusions and limitations of the life you have settled for. Come home to me."

You might notice a sense of wrongness with the life you're living. A lack of fulfilment. A series of difficult, repeating situations, like having the same kind of painful relationships or going through a string of unsatisfying jobs, until these individual moments begin to add up and form a pattern. When you're quiet and still, without distractions, you will hear it. It might be a discomfort, like wearing clothes that don't fit, or it might be a shout that things have to change.

Once upon a time, everyone knew these things. These truths were baked into most cultures. But we don't know it. We're far too busy for all this deep mysterious stuff. We've got bills to pay, errands to run, jobs to manage, hundreds of demands to juggle at any one moment. And nobody ever told us this stuff. Nothing prepared us for the need to go on a journey to find ourselves and our true potential. We were prepared for maths, and English, and history. We were prepared for fitting in, behaving ourselves, being accepted. We learn how to hold down a job, how to manage money, how to book holidays. But for most people there's no training to ask the deeper questions. We learn our life lessons from our parents and our teachers and our peers and from TV, and we apply them to our lives as best we can, and even as they fail over and over to bring us what we need from life, we keep using them because they're all we know.

That's most people, most of the time.

Something has to happen to shake us out of our comfort zone and give us a glimpse of another world. Some disruptive event. If we're lucky this comes from a mentor, or a conversations at a work conference, or the kind words of a friend. More often, it's moments of crisis, like the death of someone very important to you, or the end of a relationship, or the failure and heartbreak when something that really matters to you comes to an end. It can also be illness, or a sudden loss of security, or travelling to another culture. Maybe it's when we become parents. Maybe it's reaching a certain age and being confronted with mortality.

Something shakes us. Something makes us reassess. Almost everyone I know who's undertaken this journey had a moment like this, something that made them fundamentally questions their assumptions and ask if their beliefs actually make sense, actually belong to them.

After this disruption, the journey can begin. It doesn't always. A lot of people shake off the shock and try to put their lives back into exactly the shape it had before, even if it feels hollow and uncomfortable. If you manage to do this, people will congratulate you. Our whole culture is built around comfort zones. Find yours. Build walls around it. Don't leave it. Don't rock the boat.

But if you refuse to listen, if you follow this thirst for wholeness, then it's time for your journey towards yourself, towards *Arete*.

The Hero's Journey

When Joseph Campbell wrote about his worldwide journeys, visiting indigenous cultures and learning about their myths and traditions, he realised that there was a common story being played out in every one. He called it the Hero's Journey. Today it's really well known and you'll find all sorts of people using it in their work, from therapists to movie directors to marketing executives. Our brains enjoy the Hero's Journey structure. It evolved alongside us and we instinctively find it satisfying. However, even though it pops up in many movies and is used to sell you things, its original purpose was to help someone navigate their own personal journeys of self-discovery.

The Hero's Journey structure looks like this:

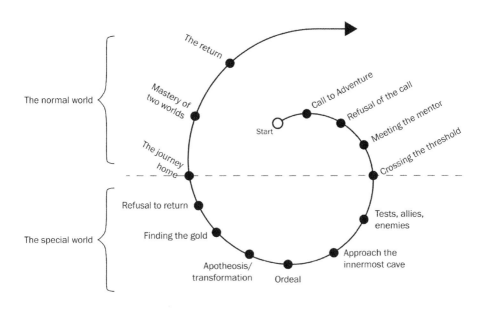

In terms of this ultimate journey towards *Arete*, the call is whatever disruptive event shook up your life enough for you to notice how wrong things feel. From there, you can see the steps that lie ahead. If you've been on your journey for a while, perhaps you can see where you've already been?

We also undertake multiple journeys in our lifetimes. Bill Plotkin, in his book *Nature and the Human Soul*, suggests that if we're free to follow our hearts and our calling, we will do this 8 times in our lives. For most of us, we only manage one or two, and usually we only manage to do it unconsciously, adapting to a suddenly different life. For example, when you first leave home.

This series is about doing it consciously, which is much more difficult and much more effective.

When the journey fails

This is difficult stuff. Everyone has so much programming and baggage that finding your way through it all can seem impossible at times. At every step, people and influences around you will be telling you to stop. They'll tell you that you're being irrational. They'll ask why you're acting different. They'll laugh at you for the books you're reading, or the places you're going, or the professionals you're hiring.

Inside, you will yearn for things to be easier. Things used to be easier, surely you can just go back? There will be a constant temptation to just go back to old habits.

In an ideal world, with the right culture around you, in the right place and with the right support, you can complete this journey in months. Most of us won't do this work in months. It's going to be a long journey, with pauses and gaps and sometimes we'll get stuck in difficult spots for a long time before we find our way through. Sometimes we'll regret ever starting, even though we know that we never had any choice.

This series is written to be a companion on your journey. Book 1 exists to make sure you have the fundamentals in place, like an understanding of masking, the aspects of self and developing compassionate non-judgement. Book 2 is the core lessons that everyone needs to complete their journey. Book 3 is how to integrate these lessons into your new life.

The world is full of people who know that this journey exists, who had their wakeup call, but something stopped them from completing their journey. Maybe life was too chaotic, too disruptive or too unsafe and they had to just focus on survival. Maybe the fear of leaving the comfort zone was too strong. Maybe they didn't have any guidance, or they got bad advice, and they chose to stop moving forwards. Again, the journey isn't usually a conscious one, so these people have been through some difficult times, had some awakenings and lessons, but never had the big breakthrough that unlocked their true self and freed up their potential. So they tend to be bitter about it, or fed up, or resentful.

A lot of people, then, never complete the Hero's Quest and find their higher plane, their *Arete*.

Adulthood and the death of innocence

Our full power lies in our full adulthood. As we will go on to explore, our culture does not provide a mechanism to move smoothly from childhood to adulthood. We slowly morph from one to the other, and usually carry with us all sorts of incomplete aspects of a confused and bewildered child self. We will need to put this inner child in a place of care and love, and remove him or her from the driving seat, if we want to take full control of our lives. We will need to assume full, adult responsibility.

This is the price of power, and your childhood innocence is something you will lose on this journey. As children, we can afford not to worry about all sorts of things because an adult is there providing for us, making sure we are safe and protected, guiding our footsteps. As we step into adulthood, it's really normal to keep doing this in all sorts of unconscious and semi-conscious ways. We ignore things, or we imagine that somebody else will sort things out for us, or we avoid doing things because they're frightening or because we might be told off, or we use friendships and relationships to create a sort of replacement parent who will nurture, guide and take responsibility for our decisions and wellbeing.

None of this is compatible with being the happy, fulfilled, powerful person you are called to become.

When we become that person, filled with awareness and personal power, there is no place for the passive handing-off of responsibility to real people or imagined people. This can be hard, at first. We are so used to living in a semi-adult state that setting childish ways aside can feel like we are losing something precious.

The theme of fully initiated adulthood runs through the whole of this book. I'll be covering what it means, how to reach it and how to maintain it. We will be exploring something called self-parenting, which is a practice that's emerged to compensate for this blending of child and adult states. We learn to identify, nurture and care for our own inner child so they feel safe and happy, allowing us to continue as empowered adults. Play and fun still happen. The person you are called to become is silly, playful, mischievous and curious. When we walk hand-in-hand with our inner child, we get to experience all these things but never lose ourselves by putting the child in the driver's seat.

Something fundamental changes in us during this journey. We lose some comforting illusions and the ability to look away from inconvenient truths. We live in direct contact with the realness of the world, with its wonders and its profound challenges. We are strong, but we are also highly conscious. This is a necessary part of the growth into the fullness of our being. You will lose your innocent ability to just close your eyes.

Commitment and stopping short

I invite you, as both your guide and as a fellow traveller, to commit to this journey, and commit to it for as long as it takes. Give yourself that gift. Let the commitment to awareness, healing, self-discovery and unlocking the limits of your potential be a lifelong commitment. As we learn and grow, as we seek heal and reconcile our past, as we take risks and discover new possibilities for ourselves, we take steps on the journey. It isn't about reaching a destination where everything is perfect and we get to put our feet up in the knowledge that we've finally arrived. Ultimately, this is about living for the journey itself, for the thrill of being alive. It's about always seeking, always wondering, always learning more about being, doing and relating.

In the next book we're going to cover the core lessons necessary to navigate the journey, and in book 3 we'll be creating a sustainable life that will make sure you don't lose the progress you've made. I call this way of being *Arete*. Abraham Maslow called it 'self-actualization', and he also observed that a certain kind of lifestyle becomes essential to people who have found it. He said:

"Self-actualizing people are, without one single exception, involved in a cause outside their own skin, in something outside themselves. They are devoted, working at something, something is very precious to them, some calling or vocation in the old sense, the priestly sense.

They are working at something which fate has called them to somehow and which they work at and which they love, so that the work–joy dichotomy in them disappears."

You may meet hard things in yourself or in the world on your path. Your commitment now will help in those times. Your dedication will compel you to persist in learning, growing and healing. Your curiosity will allow you to play and dance with problems instead of becoming too entrenched or too one-dimensional in your approach.

You may get distracted by life. That's ok. As soon as you're able, return to the path.

You may reach a certain point, perhaps when you've achieved your current goals, and decide that's far enough. That's ok. Enjoy that new place in your life, re-evaluate, explore it. But sooner or later you will be called back to the journey, or you'll long for a new goal, a new adventure or a new achievement. That's the nature of the journey. You will, along the way, find your true self and mould your life to perfectly suit your needs. But the journey itself, and a lifestyle pointed towards constant learning and growing, is *Arete*.

We'll discover the layers of that life, the skills it provides and the things it demands of you, in book 2, The 12 Rules of Happiness.

Please leave an Amazon review

It would be enormously helpful if you would leave a review for this book on Amazon.

Self-published authors like myself depend on Amazon reviews, so please consider heading to Amazon now and leaving a review.

Get your free sample of book 2, The 12 Rules of Happiness

In the next book, I share the 12 core lessons I've learned about building a sustainably happy life.

If you'd like to read the first chapter for free now, please scan this code with your phone:

Bibliography

Recommended books

Attachment Theory: A Guide to Strengthening the Relationships in Your Life by Thais Gibson (2020)

Coming Back to Life: The Updated Guide to the Work That Reconnects by Joanna Macy, Molly Young Brown, et al. (2014)

Daring Greatly: How the Courage to Be Vulnerable Transforms the Way We Live, Love, Parent, and Lead by Brené Brown (2015)

Die Wise: A Manifesto for Sanity and Soul by Stephen Jenkinson (2015)

Endgame Vol.1: The Problem of Civilization: The Problem of Civilization and Endgame Vol.2: Resistance by Derrick Jensen (2006)

Finding Earth, Finding Soul: The Invisible Path to Authentic Leadership by Tim Macartney (2007)

Fix the System, Not the Women by Laura Bates (2023)

How to Be an Adult: A Handbook on Psychological and Spiritual Integration by David Richo (1991)

Iron John: A Book About Men by Robert Bly (1990, repub 2001)

King Warrior Magician Lover: Rediscovering the Archetypes of the Mature Masculine by Robert Moore and Douglas Gillette (1992)

Making Habits, Breaking Habits: How To Make Changes That Stick by Jeremy Dean (2013)

Nonviolent Communication — A Language of Life by Marshall B. Rosenberg (2003, repub 2015)

Self-Parenting: The Complete Guide to Your Inner Conversations by John K Pollard and Linda Nusbaum (1987, repub 2018)

Soil and Soul, Alastair McIntosh (2004)

Soulcraft: Crossing into the Mysteries of Nature and Psyche by Bill Plotkin (2003)

The 7 Habits of Highly Effective People by Stephen R. Covey (1989, repub 1999)

The Body Keeps the Score: Mind, Brain and Body in the Transformation of Trauma by Bessel van der Kolk (2015)

The Hero with A Thousand Faces (The Collected Works of Joseph Campbell) by Joseph Campbell (2012)

The Language of Emotions: What Your Feelings are Trying to Tell You by Karla McLaren (2010)

The Way of the SEAL: Think Like an Elite Warrior to Lead and Succeed by Mark Divine and Allyson Edelhertz Machate (2016)

The Wild Edge of Sorrow: Rituals of Renewal and the Sacred Work of Grief by Francis Weller (2015)

Wild Power: Discover the Magic of Your Menstrual Cycle and Awaken the Feminine Path to Power by Alexandra Pope and Sjanie Hugo Wurlitzer (2017)

Wild: An Elemental Journey by Jay Griffiths (2008)

Works consulted

A Game Free Life: The definitive book on the Drama Triangle and Compassion Triangle by Stephen B. Karpman M.D. (2014)

A Little Book on the Human Shadow by Robert Bly and William Booth (1988)

Dark Side of the Light Chasers: Reclaiming your power, creativity, brilliance, and dreams by Debbie Ford (2001)

How to Be a Stoic: Using Ancient Philosophy to Live a Modern Life by Massimo Pigliucci (2017)

Meeting the Shadow: Hidden Power of the Dark Side of Human Nature (New Consciousness Reader) by Connie Zweig and Jeremiah Abrams (1990)

The Children's Fire: Heart Song of a People by Mac Macartney (2018)

The current status of urban-rural differences in psychiatric disorders, Acta Psychiatr Scand. 2010 Feb;121(2):84-93

The Outsider (Penguin Modern Classics) by Albert Camus and Sandra Smith (1942, repub 2013)

The Sickness Unto Death: A Christian Psychological Exposition of Edification and Awakening by Anti-Climacus (Classics) by Soren Kierkegaard and Alastair Hannay (1849, repub 1989)

Unlimited Power: The New Science of Personal Achievement by Tony Robbins (2001)

About the Author

Alexander Butler is a Master Life Coach, author and philosopher based in Brighton, England. He grew up in rural Cornwall, moving to London for college and then calling many places home as he trained, studied and grew his coaching business.

Today he is a busy coach with an eclectic range of international clients. He coaches every day, seeking to learn from every session and constantly challenge his ideas and assumptions about the world. His major achievements to date include setting up a café and therapy centre, coaching clients at sea on an 18th century sailing barge, and defying his philosophy lecturer's prediction that "you'll never earn any money with this degree".

He intends to continue inspiring healing and growth in his clients, to step deeper into the wild mystery of life, and eventually to found an ecovillage and training centre.

Printed in Great Britain
by Amazon

43075771R00106